SIMPLY DONE WELL DONE

SIMPLY DONE WELL DONE

Aaron McCargo, Jr.

with Mary Goodbody
Photography by Lucy Schaeffer

John Wiley & Sons, Inc.

This book is printed on acid-free paper. ♾

Food styling by Simon Andrews
Prop styling by Amy Wilson
Designed by Waterbury Publications, Inc., Des Moines, Iowa
Published by John Wiley & Sons, Inc., Hoboken, New Jersey
Published simultaneously in Canada

Library of Congress Cataloging-in-Publication Data:
McCargo, Aaron.
Simply done well done / Aaron McCargo, Jr. with Mary Goodbody ; photography by Lucy Schaeffer.
p. cm.
Includes index.
ISBN 978-0-470-61533-1
1. Cooking. I. Goodbody, Mary. II. Title.
TX714.M27 2010
641.5--dc22
2010026278
ISBN: 978-0-470-61533-1; ISBN: 978-0-470-94562-9 (ebk);
ISBN: 978-0-470-94563-6 (ebk); ISBN: 978-0-470-94564-3 (ebk)
Printed in the United States of America

10 9 8 7 6 5 4 3 2 1

I DEDICATE THIS BOOK to my first sous chef: my oldest son, Joshua McCargo. When he was younger, Joshua and I cooked together, and I remember the fun we had. Joshua, with his good looks and sense of humor, and I, with my love for bold flavors, made an awesome comedic team. Despite the challenges he currently faces, I am confident that the passion Joshua has for cooking will steer him back to the culinary field and back to the stand-up routine we created in the kitchen. Son, I love you, and I can't wait until we are in the kitchen again, side by side and making culinary magic.

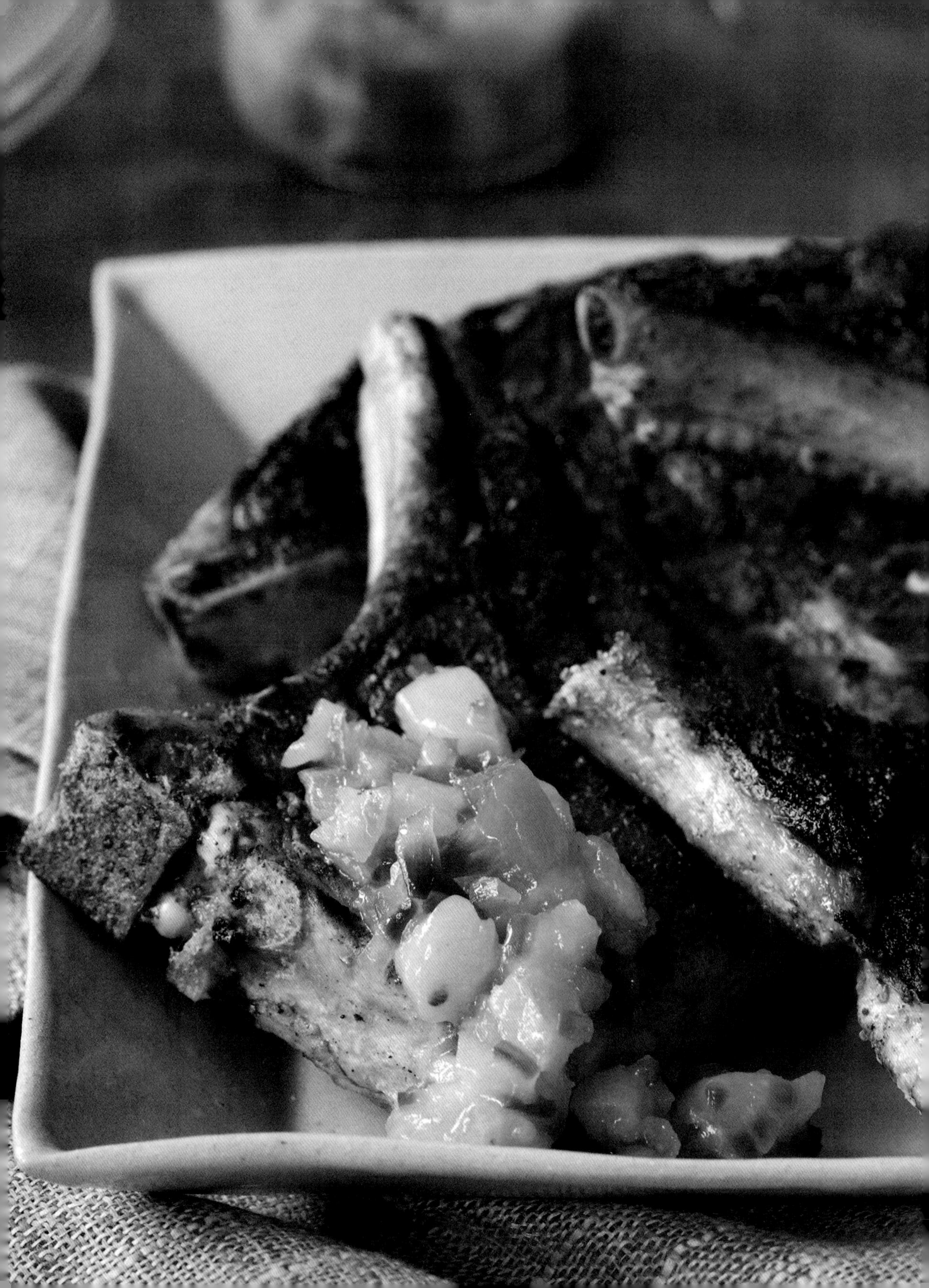

CONTENTS

ACKNOWLEDGMENTS & THANK YOUS

FIRST, I WOULD LIKE TO THANK GOD, for without Him and the gift that He gave me none of this would be possible. I would like to thank my wife, Kimberly, and my children, Joshua, Justin, and Jordan. I can't tell you how much I appreciate your patience and support. It's been an interesting journey, and I'm glad you are along to share it.

In addition, I want to thank:

Aaron, Sr., and Julia McCargo
My brothers and sisters, Vang, Carla, Andrew, Brad, and Donavan
The McCargo family
Thanks to my nieces Ashlee Matthews, Victoria Matthews, and Jessica McCargo for helping with the recipe development. Thanks to Jonathan Jernigan and the top six students of the Cathedral Kitchen Culinary Arts Program, class of 2009: James Workman, Dionne Matthews, Lebron Harvey, Adriel Lopez, and Lynn and Jose Fontanez.

Thanks also to:
My Dawg, aka Pastor, Ronald King, Sr.
Eric E. Hansen
My D-2 partner in culinary crime, Phil Falsone
Jill Falsone
Alberto Nieves
Justin Schwartz
Robert Flutie and staff
Jane Dystel and staff
Mary Goodbody
Mike and Cherrie
Jayson Belford
Doug Miller
Ian Russo, aka Salt
Pop, aka Jimmy Cosby, and Brenda
Old Dirty, aka Kevin Gaines
Debra Taplin
Al and Michelle Woods
Scott and Stephanie Shanklin
Wayne and Wanise Tally
Tank and Wanda Williams
Orion and Cheryl Joyner
Art and Victoria Loften
Special thanks to A'Driane Dudley, for taking pictures of my food that make me salivate and Lucy Schaeffer for the gorgeous photos in this book
My brother-in-law Steve, for shooting my video for NFNS
Living Hope Christian Center Family
Jefferson Hospital
Cooper Hospital
Food Network
Cathedral Kitchen, for the use of your facility
Carmen's Hoagies, for feeding me, the Big Daddy, Yellow Submarine and the Jug Handle
Cape May Atlantic Community College's Academy of Culinary Arts
The staff of We Cater to You: Stephanie Smith, Pat Hansen, the Blair family, and the late Barbara Blair
Marlton Tavern—you know what you have done for me.
Habeeb and Erica Saliu
Betty Johnson

INTRODUCTION

I WROTE THIS BOOK SO THAT I COULD SHARE MY RECIPES WITH EVERYONE WHO HAS OVER THE YEARS ASKED FOR THEM.

IT'S ALSO FOR ANYONE who may not know much about me but who just loves! loves! loves! to put boldly flavored, well-cooked, and familiar food on the table.

Who doesn't fall into this category?

This is how I cook. I coax the essence of a dish over the top, so that the food absolutely shouts with intensity and playfulness. I jack up just about everything I make—and by this I mean that I take the flavors to such heights that the final dish is totally exciting, yet without becoming a caricature of itself.

Ultimately, this is what I hope you will experience when you cook from Simply Done, Well Done. If your family is anything like mine, you will all fall in love with these recipes. I have a wife, three kids, five brothers and sisters, and numerous nieces and nephews, all with impressively sensitive palates, and they let me know when something I have cooked is spectacular—and also when it certainly is not! My siblings and I talk about what flavors we love, what we would like to try, and what we remember savoring from long-ago childhood meals.

As you read through the recipes, you will notice references to my sisters and brothers, who often drop by the house just before dinnertime or at other times toting some food that they want me to cook. I have created some of my best meals during these impromptu cooking sessions. I love to experiment with flavors and foods that appeal to my wife Kim and me. Even my young children voice their preferences and have inspired me to culinary peaks.

A Little About Me

You may know me from my Food Network show called *Big Daddy's House.* I got the show by winning *The Next Food Network Star* competition in 2008, an experience that was nothing short of incredible. Before I auditioned for the show, I was the executive chef of catering for Thomas Jefferson University Hospital in Philadelphia, where I helped the hospital plan events and occasionally developed recipes for patients with special needs. My wife, Kimberly, suggested that I enter the contest and so, on a whim, I did. I was thrilled when I was invited to participate and blown away when I won. Since then, life has been a mad race to a nonexistent finish line!

I no longer go to a nine-to-five job, five days a week, but instead work pretty much constantly. I tape the show, travel for personal appearances, participate in fund-raisers, and attend more meetings than I ever imagined. The only downside is that I am away from my family more than I like, but on the other hand, when I get time off, it's apt to be for several days at once, which gives me time to hang with Kim and my kids. And did I mention that my brothers and sisters, who live nearby, are always popping in? It's a busy life, and I thrive on it!

I was born and raised in Camden, New Jersey, a somewhat downtrodden city across the Delaware River from Philadelphia. Both my parents cooked,

MY PARENTS COOKED FOR US NEARLY EVERY DAY. WE DIDN'T EAT A LOT OF FAST FOOD OR OTHER JUNK AND I AM ETERNALLY GRATEFUL FOR THIS.

and while food was not the centerpiece that it is in my own family, it was something my brothers and sisters and I were totally into. As growing kids, we were always eager for the next meal and usually tucked into what was put in front of us with happy appreciation. My parents cooked for us nearly every day. We didn't eat a lot of fast food or other junk, and I am eternally grateful for this. To this day, I much prefer home-cooked meals to any others. You know exactly what is in the dish and you can control how it tastes.

I have been fascinated by cooking for as long as I can remember. My mother tells me I started to "help" her in the kitchen when I was very young. When I was four years old, I started baking cakes in my sister's Easy-Bake Oven. When I turned 13, I signed up as a junior volunteer in the kitchen at Cooper University Hospital in Camden. From there, my entrepreneurial spirit set in, and I began making and selling cakes to my childhood friends. I eventually studied at Atlantic Cape Community College's Academy of Culinary Arts and then went on to work in local restaurants in South Jersey and around Philadelphia.

In 2003, a childhood friend, Alberto Nieves, and I opened McCargo's Restaurant in downtown Camden. Alberto had always believed in my cooking, and it seemed fitting that we would go into the restaurant business together. It was a bistro-style eatery across the street from the courthouse and the post office. We also were not too far from the downtown campuses of Rutgers and Rowan universities. We had a lot of walk-in traffic and a good number of regulars, mostly for lunch, when lines formed outside our door and down the sidewalk. I also owned a more casual place about two blocks away called Da Spot, which the college kids liked. I had to close both places in 2005, in part because of business differences with my partners and, in the case of Da Spot, because of crime in the neighborhood.

I learned a lot from these experiences. I realized how tough the restaurant business is; at the same time, it reinforced how much I love making food that others like to eat. On these pages you will find some of my favorite and best recipes from those days and since. Enjoy them!

My Kitchen, Your Kitchen

These recipes are written for the home cook and the everyday kitchen. I don't expect you to have any special equipment or fancy appliances. I don't, and I do just fine. And yet, there are some items that are pretty much standard for every home cook.

Pots and pans

First, invest in some good pots and pans, if you have not done so already. These don't need to match or even be a full set, but they should be heavy and durable with tight-fitting lids. Everyone should own:

- 2-quart saucepan with a lid
- 9- to 10-inch skillet (I like nonstick)
- 12- to 14-inch skillet (I like nonstick)
- 8- to 12-quart stockpot or similar deep, heavy pot with a lid
- rectangular baking dish made of tempered glass or metal
- heavy-gauge roasting pan with removable rack
- heavy-gauge baking (cookie) sheet (I like nonstick)
- baking pan (jelly roll pan) measuring 10 x 15 inches with shallow rims
- Large casserole (Dutch oven) with a tight-fitting lid

Appliances

When it comes to appliances, beyond a working stove and oven, as well a good refrigerator with a freezer, I suggest you find the cash for the following:

- food processor
- hand-held electric mixer
- good quality blender
- panini press (if you like sandwiches as much as I do)
- countertop grill (I use a George Foreman grill)
- deep-fat fryer

If you don't have a deep-fat fryer, you can always use a casserole or stockpot to heat the oil. Just be sure the pot you choose is heavy and deep.

Knives

Knives are critical kitchen tools. I can't emphasize enough how important good ones are. You don't have to spend a small fortune, but with three or four sharp, well balanced knives, you will enjoy cooking far more than you

THESE RECIPES ARE WRITTEN FOR THE HOME COOK
AND THE EVERYDAY KITCHEN. I DON'T EXPECT YOU
TO HAVE ANY SPECIAL EQUIPMENT.

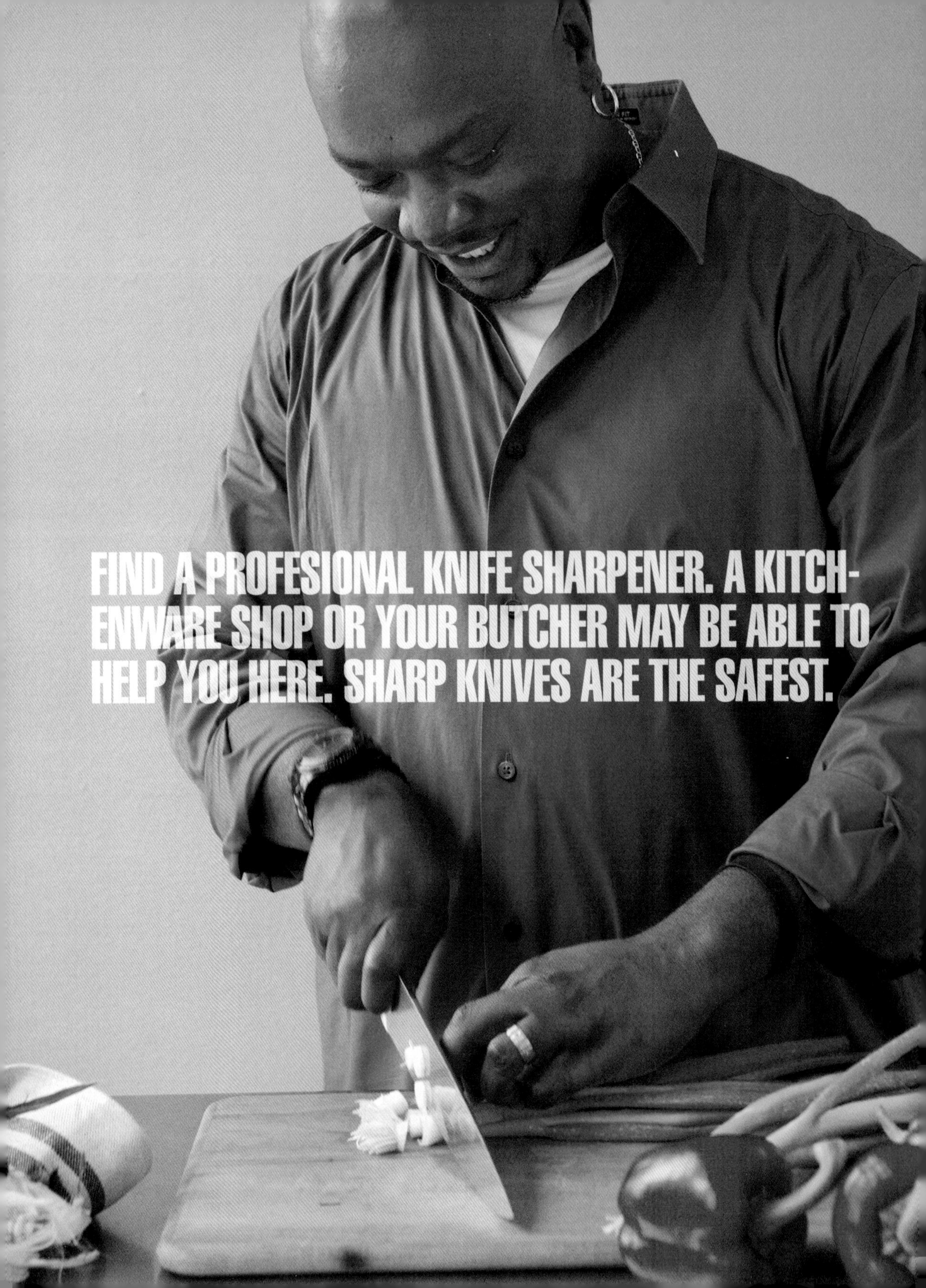
FIND A PROFESIONAL KNIFE SHARPENER. A KITCH-
ENWARE SHOP OR YOUR BUTCHER MAY BE ABLE TO
HELP YOU HERE. SHARP KNIVES ARE THE SAFEST.

ever imagined. These are a life-long investment if properly cared for, and one you will appreciate day after day. At the very minimum, you will need:

- 8- to 10-inch chef's knife
- 3- to 4-inch paring knife
- 8-inch serrated bread knife
- slicing knife

I also like 6- to 8-inch utility knives, boning knives, and a carving knife. Keep your knives sharp by honing them regularly on the sharpening steel (the long, cylindrical tool that comes with knife sets) and sharpening them periodically. To maintain the best blade, find a professional knife sharpener. A kitchenware shop or your butcher may be able to help you here. Sharp knives are the safest.

Treat your knives with respect: don't put them in the dishwasher where they can bang around, don't store them in a drawer with other utensils, and use them on the right surfaces, such as cutting boards.

Miscellaneous

Otherwise, stock your kitchen with:

- sturdy wooden spoons
- slotted spoon
- long-handled tongs
- a spatula
- 2 or 3 whisks of varying size
- oven mitts
- an instant-read thermometer
- meat thermometer
- deep-fat thermometer
- oven thermometer (to make sure your oven's temperature is accurate)
- 3 to 4 mixing bowls or various sizes (a nest of bowls works well)
- 2 to 3 plastic or wood cutting boards

You're good to go!

I love the sense of community good food engenders as much as I love cooking and creating dishes that taste just as I like them. I want you to have the same joyful experience in the kitchen and at the table and with those you love. What could be better? Have fun with these recipes. And God bless you.

APPETIZERS WITH GUSTO

APPETIZERS, FIRST COURSES, HORS D'OEUVRES— whatever you choose to call them, everyone loves them. As harbingers of the meal to come, few foods say "Welcome!" as eloquently and warmly.

I am not a formal guy; I like meals to be casual affairs for family and good friends of every generation. For me, it's as much about community as it is about food. But this does not mean I don't consider what to serve in order to get the gathering off to a good start. I do! I put a lot of thought into the appetizers. If they make everyone happy, chances are the rest of the meal will too. And that's what it's all about.

A few of the recipes in this chapter could double as light meals, others as good-time snacks, and still others are precisely what they are meant to be: first courses. All are bursting with flavor and texture. If there are kids in the mix, make the Broccoli Cheese Balls (page 23) or Mushroom-Chicken-Cheese Balls (page 28). They might go for the Pork Empanadas with Ranchero Sauce (page 34), too. Everyone will love the Deep-Fried Artichoke Hearts (page 40) and Spicy Beef Quesadillas (page 22), and seafood lovers will be as wild as I am for the Spicy Mini Salmon Croquettes with Cilantro Mayonnaise (page 27), the Spicy Steamed Mussels with Tomato and Basil (page 44), and the Fried Calamari with Lemon-Pepper-Garlic Mayonnaise (page 45).

Some of these appetizers should be made right before serving, while others can be prepared ahead of time—or elements of the dish can be made ahead. As with all recipes, read through them before you begin to cook, so that you won't be caught off guard by bad timing or missing ingredients.

Here's to the beginning of the meal, which is the time and place to serve small morsels of rich and tasty food that whet the appetite for bigger things to come.

RECIPES

BACON, GOAT CHEESE, AND DATE SPREAD WITH BAGUETTE SLICES

Just because this spread is seriously elegant, don't think it doesn't pack a punch; it does! The salty, sweet, and tart flavors happily complement one another and make this spread just right to accompany a glass of wine enjoyed in front of the fireplace in the winter or by the grill in the summer. Spread this on multigrain bread with lettuce and sliced red onion for a delicious sandwich that's perfect for lunch.

Serves 6 to 8

- 4 ounces goat cheese, softened
- 4 ounces cream cheese, softened
- ¼ cup finely diced dates
- 2 cups diced cooked chicken breast
- 8 slices applewood-smoked bacon, cooked until crispy and crumbled
- 2 tablespoons chopped scallions, white and green parts
- ½ French baguette, cut into 2-inch-thick slices

TO PREPARE: In a large bowl, stir together the cheeses and dates until the dates are thoroughly incorporated and the spread is as smooth as possible. (Alternatively, you can use a hand-held electric mixer.) Add the chicken, bacon, and scallions and fold gently just until combined. Spread on the baguette slices and serve. If not serving right away, cover and refrigerate for up to 3 days.

SPICY BEEF QUESADILLAS

Short ribs are nothing short of delicious, and when I cook them, I usually make more than we can eat at a single meal. This means that I always look for ways to use the full-flavored leftovers—and as with most braised foods, short ribs taste better the next day—and so I was excited when I spiced up the beef and then wrapped it in flour tortillas. This is a terrific appetizer and also a wonderful snack or quick lunch. You can tame the spiciness to suit your family's tastes.

Serves 4 to 6; makes 32 quesadilla triangles

- 2 tablespoons unsalted butter
- 1 cup finely diced onion
- 1 cup finely diced green bell pepper
- ½ cup chopped scallions, white and green parts
- 2 tablespoons diced chipotle chile peppers in adobo sauce
- 2 tablespoons crushed red pepper flakes
- 1 tablespoon smoked paprika
- 1 teaspoon salt
- 1 teaspoon freshly ground black pepper
- 8 ounces (about ¼ recipe) Shredded Beef Short Ribs (page 24)
- 1½ cups grated Monterey Jack cheese
- 1½ cups shredded cheddar cheese
- Eight 8-inch flour tortillas
- ½ cup olive oil
- 1½ tablespoons unsalted butter, for frying, optional

TO PREPARE: In a medium skillet, melt the butter over medium-high heat. When hot, add the onion, bell pepper, scallions, chipotle peppers, red pepper flakes, paprika, salt, and black pepper. Cook, stirring, until the vegetables begin to soften and are fragrant, 4 to 5 minutes. Remove the pan from the heat and set aside to cool slightly.

In a large bowl, mix together the shredded beef, cheeses, and the cooled vegetable mixture. Spoon equal portions of the filling on one half of each tortilla. Fold the tortillas in half and brush each side with the oil.

Put the folded tortillas, in batches, in a heated panini press or countertop grill, close the lid, and cook until heated through and the cheese melts, about 3 minutes. (Alternatively, melt about 1½ tablespoons of unsalted butter in a 12-inch nonstick skillet over medium-high heat. When the butter melts, put 2 tortillas in the pan, lower the heat to medium, and cook until the filling is hot, 2 to 3 minutes per side. Repeat with the remaining 6 quesadillas, in batches.)

Cut each quesadilla into 4 wedges and serve.

BROCCOLI CHEESE BALLS

My six-year-old son loves broccoli. In fact, he likes all vegetables, and so I came up with these cheese-packed broccoli balls as a kid-friendly appetizer. These are at the top of his list of favorites, but if your kids don't like broccoli, you still might get them to try these tasty little morsels.

Serves 4 or 5; makes about 16 balls

1½ cups fresh broccoli florets (about 1 pound of broccoli crowns)
1 cup shredded Colby cheese
1 cup shredded cheddar cheese
4 ounces Velveeta, shredded or chopped
½ teaspoon crushed red pepper flakes
½ teaspoon cayenne pepper
About 3 quarts canola oil
½ cup all-purpose flour
4 large eggs, lightly beaten
3 cups panko bread crumbs

TO PREPARE: Fill a saucepan about halfway with water and bring to a boil over medium-high heat. Blanch the broccoli until bright green and slightly softened, 1 to 2 minutes. Drain and let the broccoli cool. When cool enough to handle, chop the florets into small pieces, each about ¼ inch long.

In a large bowl, stir together the cheeses, red pepper flakes, and cayenne. Add the broccoli and mix well. Using your hands, form the mixture into balls about the size of cherry tomato; you will have at least 16 balls. Refrigerate for 30 minutes.

In a large, heavy pot, heat the oil over high heat until a deep-fat thermometer reaches a temperature of 375°F.

Put the flour in a shallow bowl, the eggs in another shallow bowl, and the panko in a third bowl. Dip each ball first in the flour, then the eggs, and finally the bread crumbs to coat. Using a long-handled slotted spoon, carefully submerge the balls, a few at a time, in the hot oil and cook until golden brown, 2 to 3 minutes, turning the balls in the oil to ensure even browning. Do not crowd the pot. Lift the balls from the oil with the slotted spoon and transfer to a large plate or baking sheet lined with paper towels to drain. Continue frying the balls in batches, letting the oil return to 375°F between each batch. Serve hot.

SHREDDED BEEF SHORT RIBS

Short ribs take a long time to cook. The long, slow cooking, or braising, is all about breaking down the meat's fibers so that it is fall-off-the-bone tender and can simmer for hours in its own juicy, succulent fat. You find short ribs in upscale restaurants now, although a decade or two ago they were a cut that didn't get much love. You can buy bone-in or boneless ribs. I prefer the latter because then I don't have to worry about the bones and the tendons, and the meat cooks a little more quickly—although it still needs that nice, slow braising. This recipe makes far more than you will need for the Spicy Beef Quesadillas on page 22, but the short ribs are so delicious that it's worth making a little extra. Plus, it's tricky to braise short ribs in small amounts. The cooked and cooled ribs freeze well for up to a month.

Makes about 2 pounds shredded beef

- 3 tablespoons grapeseed or canola oil
- 4 pounds boneless beef short ribs
- 1 medium onion, sliced
- 5 cloves garlic, smashed
- 1 cup ketchup
- ¾ cup beef broth
- About ⅔ cup canned condensed tomato soup (½ of a 10.75-ounce can)
- ¼ cup cider vinegar
- 2 tablespoons kosher salt
- 2 tablespoons coarsely ground black pepper

TO PREPARE: In a large Dutch oven or similar pot, heat the oil over medium-high heat. When hot, sear the short ribs until the meat is crusty and nicely browned on all sides, 5 to 6 minutes total. Lift the short ribs from the pot and set aside on a platter.

Add the onion and garlic to the pot and cook, stirring, until nicely browned, about 5 minutes. Stir in the ketchup, broth, tomato soup, and vinegar and bring to a simmer. Season to taste with salt and pepper.

Return the ribs to the pot, cover, and cook slowly over medium heat until the beef is fork-tender, about 2 hours. Remove the ribs from the pot and set aside to cool. When the ribs are cool enough to handle, shred the meat with a fork or your fingers. (Alternatively, roast the meat in a 425°F oven for about 2 hours, until tender.)

WHAT DOES IT MEAN TO BRAISE?

Braising is one of the best ways to get the most flavor from food, particularly good for cuts of relatively tough meat such as short ribs, veal shanks, and brisket. Simply, it means to simmer food slowly in a small amount of liquid. The liquid may be nothing more than water, or it might be broth, wine, beer, or a mixture of these things. Usually the braising liquid is flavored with aromatic vegetables such as onions, leeks, and garlic, and very often herbs are tossed into the pot, too. This sounds a lot like a stew (and as I said, stews are braised dishes).

Vegetables can also be braised. Commonly braised veggies are endive, leeks, and cabbage—those that are fibrous and benefit from long, moist cooking.

You can braise on top of the stove or in the oven. What you need for success is a heavy pot with a tight-fitting lid, low heat, and time. The lid is vital because it prevents the liquid from evaporating and turns the interior of the pot into a simmering steam bath, so that the food cooks in a moist environment that breaks down the fibers in the meat, poultry, or vegetables. When cooked, you may not even need a knife to cut the meat or vegetables, and the flavors will be deliciously deep and intense. Convinced?

WHAT ARE PANKO BREAD CRUMBS?

I use panko bread crumbs in many of my recipes because I love the way they adhere to food, and I appreciate their snappy little crunch. You can't make these at home; you have to buy them. They were developed by the Japanese and sometimes are called Japanese bread crumbs. The difference between them and other bread crumbs is how they are processed. Panko crumbs are flakier, with a slightly larger surface area, and thus result in crispier food. They're sold in just about every supermarket and certainly in Asian markets. If you can't find them, use regular bread crumbs.

PANKO CRUMBS ARE FLAKIER WITH A SLIGHTLY LARGER SURFACE AREA, AND THUS RESULT IN CRISPIER FOOD.

SPICY MINI SALMON CROQUETTES WITH CILANTRO MAYONNAISE

My mom used to make salmon cakes for supper when I was a kid, which she served over white rice. I liked them a lot, but as I got older and my palate became a little more developed, I decided to make them with the best canned salmon money could buy—preferably without the bones we'd find in Mom's salmon cakes. I jack up the flavor with some spice, cook it as a croquette, and serve it with dressed-up mayonnaise flavored with cilantro. Outstanding!

Serves 4 to 6; makes 16 croquettes

1 cup panko bread crumbs
¼ cup all-purpose flour
¼ cup diced shallots
¼ cup diced scallions, white and green parts
2 tablespoons chopped fresh cilantro leaves
1 large egg, lightly beaten
1 tablespoon Chesapeake Spice Blend (page 190)
1 tablespoon freshly ground coarse black pepper
1 tablespoon granulated garlic powder
Pinch of cayenne pepper
Two 16-ounce cans pink salmon, drained, any bones and skin removed
½ cup (1 stick) unsalted butter
About 2 cups Cilantro Mayonnaise (page 183)

TO PREPARE: Preheat the oven to 300°F. Set a wire rack in a shallow baking pan.

In a large bowl, stir together the bread crumbs, flour, shallots, scallions, cilantro, egg, seasoning, black pepper, garlic powder, and cayenne.

Fold the salmon into the mixture until just mixed but not mushy. With dampened hands, form the salmon mixture into 16 equal-size oval croquettes.

In a large skillet, melt about 2 tablespoons of the butter over medium-high heat. Cook the croquettes, turning them gently during cooking so that they cook evenly, until nicely browned, 2 to 3 minutes total. You will have to cook a few croquettes at a time and add more butter as needed; you may not need all the butter. As they cook, transfer the croquettes to the rack set in the pan and keep warm in the oven. Serve the warm croquettes with the mayonnaise.

MUSHROOM-CHICKEN-CHEESE BALLS

These little balls made from chicken and mushrooms are the long-lost cousins of the Broccoli Cheese Balls on page 23 and are just right for anyone who prefers meaty bites to vegetarian ones. I use canned mushrooms simply because they are so convenient, but if you want to use fresh mushrooms, go for it. Cook them in a little butter and oil until they soften and, once cooked, add them to the mixture in place of the canned. I like these chicken balls made either way, but when I use a mixture of cooked fresh cremini, shiitake, and oyster mushrooms, I find the flavor is more intense.

Serves 7 to 10; makes 24 to 32 balls

- 3 cups diced chicken (from 1 store-bought rotisserie chicken; it should weigh about 2 pounds)
- 2 cups grated sharp cheddar cheese
- 2 cups Cilantro Mayonnaise (page 183)
- ¼ cup sliced scallions, white and green parts
- One 12-ounce can sliced mushrooms, drained
- 1 jalapeño chile pepper, finely diced
- 1 teaspoon freshly ground black pepper
- 3¼ cups all-purpose flour
- 4 large eggs, lightly beaten
- 2 cups panko bread crumbs
- Vegetable oil, for frying

TO PREPARE: In a large bowl, toss the chicken with the cheese, 1½ cups of the mayonnaise, the scallions, mushrooms, jalapeño, and black pepper. Between dampened palms, roll the chicken mixture into balls weighing about 1 ounce each or measuring about 1 tablespoon. You will have between 24 and 32 balls.

Put the flour in a shallow bowl, put the eggs in another shallow bowl, and put the panko in a third. Roll each ball in the flour, then the eggs, and then the bread crumbs to coat.

Pour the oil into a deep, heavy pot to a depth of 3 to 4 inches. Heat over medium-high heat until it registers 350°F on a deep-fat thermometer. Another way to tell if the oil is hot enough is to spatter a little water on it. If the water sizzles, it's hot. You can also insert a wooden spoon or skewer in the hot oil and see if bubbles form around the spoon where it meets the oil. If so, the oil is hot.

Using a long-handled slotted spoon, carefully submerge 3 or 4 chicken balls in the hot oil. Let the chicken balls cook until golden brown, 1½ to 2 minutes. Lift them from the hot oil with the slotted spoon and transfer to a large plate or baking sheet lined with paper towels to drain. Continue frying the chicken balls in batches, letting the oil return to 350°F between each batch. Serve the hot chicken balls with the remaining ½ cup of cilantro mayonnaise.

IS THERE REALLY A DIFFERENCE AMONG KINDS OF MUSHROOMS?

White mushrooms, sold just about everywhere, bring good mushroom flavor to all sorts of dishes, but I like to experiment with other kinds because many provide richer, earthier flavor—and I'm all about tapping into a world of flavor. Worldwide there are probably thirty to forty thousand varieties of mushrooms (many of which are not safe to eat), so it's not surprising that an array of different ones turn up at supermarkets and farmers' markets. There are a lot to choose from! You can use any mushrooms in place of any other if you are interested in exploring flavors and textures.

Cremini are the most common brown mushrooms sold in stores and are a little more intense than white mushrooms. When they mature, they turn into portobellos, which are large, meaty mushrooms that I just love. Many of these mushrooms are called "wild mushrooms," although nearly all are cultivated nowadays. Some of my favorites are morels, oysters, and shiitakes.

BACON-WRAPPED SAUSAGES WITH CASHEWS

My baby sister Carla stopped by one day, as she and my other siblings are in the habit of doing fairly regularly. She brought some cashews with her to snack on, but when she saw the hot sausage on a roll that I was eating, she decided she wanted some of what I had. Instead of sharing my meal with her, I took the nuts, tossed them with sugar, and then wrapped them and some sausage in bacon and stuck it in the oven. We both drooled over the result! Ever since, she has been bringing food to the house to challenge me.

Serves 4 to 6; makes 32 pieces

- 12 slices par-cooked bacon (see Note below)
- 1 cup packed dark brown sugar
- 1 cup coarsely chopped honey-roasted cashews
- 1 cup finely chopped scallions, white and green parts
- 1 teaspoon cayenne pepper
- 1 teaspoon ground cinnamon
- 8 spicy smoked beef sausages, each about 4 inches long, cut into 1-inch pieces

TO PREPARE: Preheat the oven to 400°F.

Lay the bacon slices on a baking sheet and bake for 8 to 10 minutes, or just until the bacon softens and is still limp and pliable. Drain on paper towels.

In a medium bowl, stir together the sugar, cashews, scallions, cayenne, and cinnamon.

Lay each slice of bacon on a work surface and sprinkle an equal amount of the sugar mixture along the length of the bacon. Press gently to make sure the mixture adheres to the bacon. Lay a sausage piece near the end of each bacon slice and roll the sausage in the bacon. Transfer each roll to a shallow baking pan, seam side down. Bake for 18 to 20 minutes, until the bacon is crispy and cooked through. Serve hot.

NOTE: Par-cooking, or undercooking, bacon is easy. Cook the bacon on a grill, in the oven, or in a skillet as usual, but cook it only until it's barely done, still flabby and soft.

BLT-STUFFED BELGIAN ENDIVE

Back when I owned McCargo's Restaurant in downtown Camden, across the street from the federal courthouse, a court worker regularly asked for a BLT without the bread! This blew my mind, and I kept trying to come up with ways to make him a decent sandwich without having it drip all over him. I finally came up with the idea to use endive as the "container" for the other ingredients. Success!

Serves 4

- ½ cup cream cheese, softened
- 2 cups mayonnaise
- 2 tablespoons dry ranch dressing mix
- 2 tablespoons chopped fresh chives
- ½ cup seeded, finely diced tomatoes
- 6 to 8 slices bacon, cooked until crispy and crumbled (about ¼ cup)
- 3 large heads Belgian endive
- 2 tablespoons chopped scallions, white and green parts, for garnish

TO PREPARE: In a large bowl, using a hand-held electric mixer, mix together the cream cheese, mayonnaise, ranch dressing mix, and chives. When well combined, fold in the tomatoes and bacon.

Separate the endive leaves from the heads. Dollop the mayonnaise mixture on the wide end of each endive leaf and serve garnished with scallions.

SWEET AND SPICY NUTS AND GARLICKY AND SAVORY NUTS

I love seasoned nuts. They're easy to make, they have some shelf life to them, and everyone likes them for snacking or as a light appetizer. You can use any kind of nut you like with either of these spice mixtures, but if you use the sweet and spicy mixture, prepare the nuts well ahead of serving time, as the cayenne pepper in the skillet will make people in your house cough!

YOU CAN USE ANY KIND OF NUT YOU LIKE WITH EITHER OF THESE SPICE MIXTURES. I HAVE ALSO FOUND THAT THESE NUTS ARE PRETTY KID-FRIENDLY.

SWEET AND SPICY NUTS

Serves 2 to 4; makes about 2 cups

1 tablespoon granulated sugar
1 tablespoon light brown sugar
1 teaspoon salt
½ teaspoon cayenne pepper
1 tablespoon canola oil
2 cups salted dry-roasted peanuts

TO PREPARE: In a small bowl, mix together the sugars, salt, and cayenne.

In a large, nonstick dry skillet heat the oil over medium-high heat and toast the peanuts in a single layer until lightly browned and fragrant, 6 to 8 minutes. Shake the pan several times or turn the nuts to ensure even browning.

Remove the pan from the heat, add the sugar mixture and toss lightly until the nuts are fragrant, 1 to 2 minutes. Transfer the nuts to a baking sheet and spread in an even layer to cool. Serve at room temperature. The nuts will keep for up to 5 days in an airtight container.

GARLICKY AND SAVORY NUTS

Serves 4 to 6; makes about 3 cups

2 tablespoons garlic salt
1 tablespoon granulated garlic powder
1 teaspoon kosher salt
1 teaspoon freshly ground black pepper
½ teaspoon ground cumin
½ teaspoon granulated onion powder
1 tablespoon canola oil
3 cups shelled nuts, such as pecans, walnuts, or almonds

TO PREPARE: In a small bowl, mix together the garlic salt, garlic powder, kosher salt, black pepper, cumin, and onion powder.

In a large, nonstick dry skillet heat the oil over medium-high heat and toast the nuts in a single layer until lightly browned and fragrant, 6 to 8 minutes. Shake the pan several times or turn the nuts to ensure even browning. Remove the pan from the heat and toss the nuts with the garlic mixture. Transfer the nuts to a baking sheet and spread in an even layer to cool slightly. Serve warm. The nuts will keep for up to 5 days in an airtight container.

PORK EMPANADAS WITH RANCHERO SAUCE

Camden, New Jersey, where I grew up, has a large and vibrant Latino population. When I was a kid, I loved eating the empanadas sold in the Mexican and Spanish markets found in nearly every corner of the city. I lived in south Camden, which was a very mixed neighborhood, but I only had to cross over to east Camden for Mexican shops and restaurants and into north Camden for Puerto Rican stores. I relied on this rich history of sampling many different empanadas when I decided to create my own with a seriously spicy ranchero sauce.

Serves 6 to 8; makes about 14 empanadas

RANCHERO SAUCE:

3 tablespoons olive oil
½ medium onion, chopped
2 tablespoons minced garlic
One 15-ounce can diced fire-roasted tomatoes
One 6-ounce can diced green chiles
1 chipotle chile pepper in adobo sauce, minced
1 teaspoon salt
1 teaspoon freshly ground black pepper
½ bunch fresh cilantro, chopped

EMPANADAS:

½ pound pork tenderloin, cut into small cubes
Salt and freshly cracked black pepper
2 tablespoons olive oil
3 scallions, sliced, white and green parts
2 chipotle chile peppers in adobo sauce, minced
1 cup grated smoked cheddar cheese
¼ cup chopped fresh cilantro
Two 9-inch unbaked, store-bought pie dough rounds
2 large eggs, lightly beaten

TO PREPARE: Preheat the oven to 425°F. Line a shallow baking pan, such as a jelly-roll pan or a baking sheet, with parchment paper.

recipe continued on page 36

TO MAKE THE RANCHERO SAUCE: In a medium saucepan, heat the oil over medium-high heat. When hot, add the onion and garlic and cook, stirring, until softened, 2 to 3 minutes. Add the tomatoes, chiles, and chipotle pepper and cook, stirring to blend the flavors. Add the salt and black pepper and cook until the sauce reduces slightly, 3 to 4 minutes. Stir in the cilantro and set aside, covered, to keep warm.

TO MAKE THE EMPANADAS: Season the pork with salt and black pepper. In a large skillet, heat the oil over medium-high heat. When hot, sear the pork cubes, turning occasionally, until lightly browned, 3 to 5 minutes. Transfer the cubes of meat to a shallow bowl and let them cool slightly. Add the scallions, chipotle peppers, cheddar, and cilantro to the bowl and toss well.

On a lightly floured surface, roll the pie rounds so that they are slightly larger and a little thinner (about ⅛ inch thick). Using a 3-inch round biscuit cutter, punch out circles of dough.

Put about 2 tablespoons of the filling, off center, on each round of dough. Brush the edges of the dough with the beaten egg and fold it over the filling to form a half-moon shape. Crimp the edges closed with a fork and arrange the empanadas on the prepared baking sheet. Bake for 13 to 15 minutes or until nicely browned. Serve warm with the ranchero sauce for dipping.

WHEN I WAS A KID, I LOVED EATING THE EMPANADAS SOLD IN THE MEXICAN AND SPANISH MARKETS FOUND IN NEARLY EVERY CORNER OF THE CITY.

CORDON BLEU–STYLE FRITTERS WITH DIJON MUSTARD–GRUYÈRE CHEESE SAUCE

These fritters are among my favorites, especially when served with the mustard-Gruyère sauce. While I suggest Swiss cheese as a substitute for the Gruyère in the sauce recipe, try to use Gruyère here if at all possible; its bite goes so well with the fritters. If you have extra sauce, don't toss it. Consider yourself lucky, because it's great with Tempting Tempura-Fried Okra (page 39), Spicy Mini Salmon Croquettes (page 27), or Deep-Fried Artichoke Hearts (page 40). Once you try these fritters, you might decide to serve them as a light main course, although they are an excellent first course or appetizer.

Serves 4 to 6; makes about 24 fritters

- 2 tablespoons olive oil
- ½ cup minced Serrano ham or another good cured ham
- ½ cup diced roasted deli turkey
- One 5-ounce can chicken, drained
- 1 medium onion, finely chopped
- ⅔ cup self-rising flour
- ⅔ cup chicken broth
- 2 large eggs, lightly beaten
- ½ teaspoon smoked paprika
- Salt and freshly ground black pepper
- Canola oil, for frying
- Dijon Mustard–Gruyère Cheese Sauce (page 187)

TO PREPARE: In a large skillet, heat the olive oil over medium-high heat. When hot, add the ham, turkey, chicken, and onion and cook, stirring, until the meat is slightly softened, about 3 minutes. Remove from the heat and let the meat mixture cool in the pan.

Put the flour in a large bowl and, stirring constantly, slowly add the broth until the mixture is smooth and creamy. Stir in the eggs and paprika. Add the cooled meat mixture and any oil from the skillet to the batter and season lightly with salt and pepper.

Pour the canola oil into a large skillet to a depth of about ¼ inch and heat over medium-high heat until very hot and nearly smoking.

Form the batter into small fritters, a generous tablespoon or so each, and carefully drop them into the hot skillet in batches. Do not crowd the skillet. Cook, turning once or twice, until well browned, 1½ to 3 minutes. The fritters will be a little loose and delicate in texture, which is how they should be. Drain on paper towels and serve warm with the mustard sauce.

TEMPTING TEMPURA-FRIED OKRA

Poor okra. When it comes to vegetables, it's the one that's been left out in the rain, which is a shame because it really is tasty. When I was a kid, my mother served stewed okra pretty often, and while I liked it, the first time I fried the vegetable, I was delighted because the sliminess just disappeared. Although okra is eaten more down south than up north, there's no reason to travel to enjoy it, and frying it converts okra haters into okra lovers.

Serves 4 to 6

3 quarts canola oil
2 cups all-purpose flour
2 teaspoons salt, plus more for seasoning the okra
1 teaspoon freshly ground black pepper
1 cup club soda
1 large egg, lightly beaten
1 teaspoon cream of tartar
2 pounds fresh okra, stems trimmed and okra halved lengthwise
Sweet and Sticky Honey-Scallion Dipping Sauce (page 178)

TO PREPARE: In a large, heavy pot, heat the oil over high heat until a deep-fat thermometer reaches a temperature of 350°F.

In a large bowl, mix 1½ cups flour with the salt and pepper. Add the club soda, egg, and cream of tartar and whisk until smooth.

Coat the okra with the remaining ½ cup of flour and shake off any excess. Dip the okra in the batter and then, using a long-handled slotted spoon or tongs, carefully submerge the okra in the oil and fry until golden brown, 6 to 8 minutes. Do not crowd the pot. Lift the okra from the oil with the slotted spoon or tongs, transfer to a large plate or baking sheet lined with paper towels to drain, and season with salt while hot. Continue frying the okra, letting the oil return to 350°F between batches. Serve hot with the dipping sauce.

DEEP-FRIED ARTICHOKE HEARTS

After my sister Carla first discovered marinated artichoke hearts and started adding them to salads, she asked me for some other ideas for using them. I came up with these fried artichoke hearts, which we decided are as delish scattered over a green salad, rather like croutons, as they are dipped in a deep, heady roasted garlic mayonnaise.

Serves 4 to 6; makes about 16 pieces

1 quart canola oil

¼ cup all-purpose flour

1 tablespoon lemon-pepper seasoning

1 tablespoon kosher salt

2 large eggs, lightly beaten

2 cups panko bread crumbs

24-ounces jarred marinated artichoke hearts (four 6-ounce jars), drained

1 recipe Roasted Garlic Mayonnaise (page 179)

TO PREPARE: In a large, heavy pot, heat the oil over high heat until a deep-fat thermometer reaches a temperature of 375°F.

In a small bowl, mix the flour with the lemon-pepper seasoning and salt. Put the seasoned flour in a shallow bowl, the eggs in another bowl, and the panko in a third bowl. Dust each artichoke first in the flour, then dip in the eggs, and finally roll in the bread crumbs to coat.

Using a long-handled slotted spoon, without crowding the pot, carefully submerge the artichokes in batches in the oil and fry until golden brown, 2 to 3 minutes. Lift the artichokes from the oil with the slotted spoon and transfer to a large plate or baking sheet lined with paper towels to drain. Continue frying the artichokes in batches, letting the oil return to 375°F between batches. Serve warm with the mayonnaise for dipping on the side.

GRILLED EGGPLANT ROULADES WITH GOAT CHEESE AND DRIED CHERRIES

This eggplant roulade is just what you'll want to eat on a summer day. The lightly seasoned goat cheese is the ideal soft filling for the eggplant, and the dried cherries add the right degree of tartness. I love dried cherries—so different from dried cranberries or raisins—and they taste truly great here. I find a lot of people are intimidated by eggplant and only think to make eggplant parmesan. Eggplant is really versatile, though, as you'll discover when you try this recipe.

Serves 4 to 6; makes 10 roulades

2 large eggplants, ends trimmed (about 2 pounds each)
3 tablespoons olive oil
Salt and freshly ground black pepper
8 ounces goat cheese, softened
½ cup dried cherries
2 tablespoons chopped fresh flat-leaf parsley
2 tablespoons heavy cream
1 tablespoon coarse sea salt
1 tablespoon freshly cracked black pepper
Extra-virgin olive oil, for drizzling
White balsamic vinegar, for drizzling
1 tablespoon chopped fresh chives

TO PREPARE: Prepare a hot fire in a charcoal or gas grill and oil the grill grates, or heat a countertop grill to high. Preheat the oven to 375°F. Line a baking sheet or shallow baking pan with parchment paper.

Cut each eggplant lengthwise into ¼-inch-thick slices. You want 10 eggplant slices. Drizzle the slices with the olive oil and season lightly with salt and pepper. Grill until nicely charred, 1 to 2 minutes per side. Transfer to the prepared baking sheet, arranging them in a single layer, to cool slightly.

In a medium bowl, mix together the cheese, cherries, parsley, heavy cream, salt, and black pepper until all the ingredients are well incorporated.

Spoon 2 to 3 tablespoons of the cheese mixture on the tapered end of each eggplant slice. Roll the eggplant around the cheese mixture and return the roulades to the baking sheet. Bake for 3 to 4 minutes or until the cheese filling begins to melt slightly and the eggplant is warmed through. Transfer to a platter, drizzle with the extra-virgin olive oil and vinegar, and sprinkle with the chives.

COCONUT-GINGER CHICKEN SKEWERS WITH SRIRACHA-HONEY BUTTER

While these coconut-and-ginger-flavored chicken strips are wonderful served with the spicy butter I recommend, they also would be delicious with a peanutty satay sauce or sweet fruit dipping sauce. These skewers will disappear in minutes, regardless of whom you've invited over.

Serves 4; makes 16 skewers

3 quarts canola oil

Four 8-ounce boneless, skinless chicken breasts, each cut lengthwise into 4 strips

¼ cup all-purpose flour

1 teaspoon salt

½ teaspoon freshly ground black pepper

1½ cups panko bread crumbs

1 cup sweetened shredded coconut

3 tablespoons shredded fresh ginger

2 large eggs

Sriracha-Honey Butter (page 203), for serving

TO PREPARE: In a shallow bowl, soak 16 wooden skewers in cold water for about 20 minutes. Drain.

In a heavy, deep pot, heat the oil to 350°F over medium-high heat. Line a baking sheet or tray with parchment paper.

Thread each skewer with a chicken breast, weaving the skewer in and out of the meat. Leave a "handle" at one end of the skewers.

In a wide, shallow bowl, mix together the flour, salt, and pepper. In another bowl, mix together the panko, coconut, and ginger. In a third bowl, whisk the eggs.

Dip the chicken strips first in the flour mixture and then in the bread crumb mixture. Finally, dip them in the eggs and press the crumb mixture into the meat. Set aside on the prepared baking sheet.

Grasping the handle ends of the skewers, carefully submerge the chicken in the hot oil and fry until golden brown, 1½ to 3 minutes per side, frying only a few strips at a time. Transfer to a large plate or baking sheet lined with paper towels to drain. Continue frying the strips, letting the oil return to 350°F between batches. Serve with the seasoned butter.

SPICY STEAMED MUSSELS WITH TOMATO AND BASIL

Because I didn't eat seafood when I was a kid, I had not tasted mussels until I was an adult. I was always amazed when others ordered them in restaurants because so many of the shiny, black-shelled mollusks came piled in a large bowl for a single serving. When I started cooking them, I realized how inexpensive they were—and how great they tasted with tomato sauce. I love them now.

Serves 4

- 3 tablespoons olive oil
- 3 tablespoons minced garlic
- 2 teaspoons crushed red pepper flakes
- 1 medium onion, sliced
- 2 teaspoons dried basil
- 2 pounds fresh mussels, beards removed, rinsed well
- One 15-ounce can condensed tomato soup
- 1 cup dry white wine
- ½ cup vegetable broth
- 1 cup cherry tomatoes, halved
- 3 tablespoons chopped fresh basil
- 3 tablespoons chopped fresh flat-leaf parsley
- Juice of 1 lemon
- Salt and freshly ground black pepper
- Crusty baguettes, sliced, for serving

TO PREPARE: In a large soup pot, heat the oil over medium-high heat. When hot, add the garlic and red pepper flakes and cook, stirring, to release the flavors, 1 to 2 minutes. Add the onion and dried basil and cook, stirring, until the onion begins to soften, 1 to 2 minutes. Add the mussels and stir to coat with the vegetable mixture. Add the tomato soup, wine, and broth; stir well, bring to a simmer, cover, and cook until the mussels open, 5 to 6 minutes.

Add the cherry tomatoes, fresh basil, parsley, and lemon juice. Season to taste with salt and pepper and stir well. Discard any mussels that do not open. Ladle the mussels and broth onto a large serving platter or shallow serving dish and serve with the baguettes.

FRIED CALAMARI WITH LEMON-PEPPER-GARLIC MAYONNAISE

When I was younger, I avoided seafood because of an allergy. I seem to have outgrown the problem, which is good news for a guy who likes food as much as I do. Calamari was the first seafood I tried when I figured it was safe, and to this day it is my top choice. I prefer it with a cold sauce, such as this peppery mayonnaise, although when I order it in restaurants it nearly always comes with warm marinara sauce. Also good! If you want to serve these with marinara, turn to page 200 for my easy recipe. These calamari really have to be cooked right before serving, so that they don't lose their love.

I suggest you buy frozen calamari that is already cut into rings. If you buy whole squid, you will have to remove the head and tentacles before cleaning the body—also called the mantle—and slicing it into rings. I am sure you will arrive at the same conclusion I did: buy the squid already cleaned and sliced!

Serves 4 to 6

- 2 quarts canola oil
- 1 pound cleaned squid, cut into rings
- ½ cup Chesapeake Spice Blend (page 190)
- 1 cup cornstarch
- 3 large eggs, lightly beaten
- 1 cup cornmeal
- Salt, optional
- 1¼ cups Lemon-Pepper-Garlic Mayonnaise (page 180)

TO PREPARE: In a large, heavy pot, heat the oil over high heat until a deep-fat thermometer reaches a temperature of 375°F.

Put the calamari in a bowl, sprinkle with about half the seasoning, and toss gently to coat evenly.

In a small bowl, mix the cornstarch with the remaining ¼ cup of seasoning. Put the seasoned cornstarch in a shallow bowl, the eggs in another bowl, and the cornmeal in a third bowl. Dust the calamari first with the cornstarch and shake off the excess, and then dip the pieces in the eggs and let any excess drip off. Finally, coat the calamari with the cornmeal and shake off the excess.

Using a long-handled slotted spoon, carefully submerge the calamari in the oil and fry until golden brown, 4 to 6 minutes, without crowding the pan. Lift the calamari from the oil with the slotted spoon and transfer to a large plate or baking sheet lined with paper towels to drain. Season to taste with salt while hot, if desired. Continue frying the calamari, letting the oil return to 375°F between batches. Serve with the mayonnaise for dipping.

SAVORY TACO CHICKEN PIZZA WITH GUACAMOLE AND CHIPOTLE SALSA

A viewer sent a "Dear Food Network" question challenging me to come up with a pizza packed with loads of flavor. I love a challenge and I love tacos, so I came up with a pizza topped with all the good flavors of the Mexican specialty. These pizzas are truly addictive and simple to make. The sweet, hot, and savory flavors play off each other, and the underlying component of heat is never overwhelming.

Serves 6 to 8

2 to 3 boneless, skinless chicken breast halves (about 1 pound)
About ¼ cup Taco Blend (page 192)
¼ cup canola oil
1 pound store-bought pizza dough
¼ cup olive oil
1 cup shredded sharp cheddar cheese
1 cup shredded mozzarella cheese
1 cup Zesty Guacamole (page 198)
1 cup Chipotle Salsa (page 199)
½ cup sour cream
¼ cup chopped fresh cilantro

TO PREPARE: Using a meat mallet or the bottom of a small, heavy skillet, gently pound the chicken breasts until thin (see Note, page 117). Rub the meat with about 3 tablespoons of the taco blend and then lay the pieces in a large glass or ceramic dish and pour the canola oil over them. Turn to coat, cover, and refrigerate for about 30 minutes.

Prepare a moderately hot fire in a charcoal or gas grill and oil the grill grates.

When the grill is hot, lift the chicken from the marinade, letting any excess drip off. Grill the chicken until cooked through, about 3 minutes per side. Remove from the grill and let the chicken cool. When cool enough to handle, cut into bite-size cubes.

Meanwhile, on a lightly floured surface, cut the pizza dough into 4 equal pieces. Roll the pizza dough into thin circles, rub the dough circles on both sides with the olive oil, and dust lightly with the remaining 1 tablespoon of taco blend. Carefully transfer the dough circles to the grill and cook until crispy and lightly browned, 1 to 2 minutes per side.

Meanwhile, in a medium bowl, mix together the cheeses. While the dough is still on the grill, top the dough circles with equal amounts of cheese and then with equal amounts of chicken. Grill over a cool part of the grill, covered, until the cheese melts and is bubbling, 3 to 4 minutes. (Alternatively, bake the pizzas in a 350°F oven for 3 to 4 minutes, or until the cheese is bubbling.)

Top the pizzas with the guacamole, salsa, sour cream, and cilantro. Cut into wedges for serving.

HAM-AND-CHEESE PICKLE ROLLS

These are a takeoff on jalapeño shooters, which are a favorite bar food all around the country. These have the same saltiness and juiciness but not the heat. They are good as presented here, or you could serve them with a sliced baguette.

Serves 4 to 6; makes 16 rolls

- 1 cup diced deli-style smoked ham
- 4 ounces cream cheese, softened
- 2 tablespoons chopped fresh chives
- ½ cup Worcestershire sauce
- ½ teaspoon hot pepper sauce, such as Tabasco
- 4 or 5 whole dill pickles

TO PREPARE: In a medium bowl, stir together the ham, cream cheese, chives, Worcestershire sauce, and hot pepper sauce.

Slice the pickles lengthwise into slices about 1 inch wide, 2½ inches long, and ⅛ inch thick. Pat dry with paper towels. You need at least 16 pickle slices, but a few extra are a good idea in case some are too thick to roll.

Spoon about ¾ tablespoon of the ham mixture onto the end of each pickle slice. Roll each pickle slice around the filling and secure with a toothpick. Serve cold.

BACON AND BEAN MINI PASTRIES

My wife, Kimberly, is a serious bean-dip lover, and who can blame her? I used to make the seven-layer dip when I worked at T.G.I. Friday's years ago, and one day I took some of the puff pastry sheets we used at the restaurant for the pigs in a blanket and made mini cups for some bean dip. A first-class appetizer was born! Both Kim and I like bacon, but if you want a vegetarian appetizer, leave it out.

Serves 6 to 8; makes about 24 pastries

2 sheets frozen puff pastry, thawed
One 16-ounce can refried beans
1 pound sliced bacon, cooked until crispy and crumbled (about 1 cups)
1 pound grated or shredded cheddar cheese
¾ cup pickled jalapeño chile pepper rings (at least 24 pieces)
½ cup sour cream
¼ cup chopped scallions, white and green parts
½ cup Chipotle Salsa (page 199) or mild or spicy store-bought salsa, optional
½ cup Zesty Guacamole (page 198), optional

TO PREPARE: Preheat the oven to 325°F.

Cut the puff pastry sheets into 24 squares and press the squares into the cups of mini muffin tins. With a fork, pierce each puff pastry piece several times. Bake for 12 to 15 minutes, until golden brown. Set the muffin tins aside.

Increase the oven temperature to 400°F.

In a medium bowl, mix the beans with the bacon and spoon equal amounts of the mixture into each baked pastry shell. Top with equal amounts of cheese and bake for 6 to 8 minutes, until the cheese melts.

Top each pastry with a jalapeño slice, a dollop of sour cream, and a few scallion pieces. Serve with salsa and guacamole, if desired.

SMOOTH & HEARTY SOUPS

I JUST PLAIN LOVE SOUP AND HAVE ALWAYS BEEN GOOD AT MAKING IT. Maybe it's because I come from Camden, New Jersey, home of Campbell's Soup. When we were kids, the factory on Market Street had big windows, and you could stop outside and watch the assembly-line workers guiding the cans along the conveyor belts. My mom used to park us kids in front of those windows and tell us to count the cans while she ran a quick errand. It was a good way to keep a few children occupied for a little while! The factory is now closed, but the headquarters for the company is still in town.

I owned a restaurant called McCargo's in downtown Camden from 2003 to 2005 and always had soup on the menu—even in the summertime. My wife and I debated that decision; she wasn't sure soup would move in the summer, but Jimmy Cosby, my father-in-law, agreed with me. "Who doesn't eat soup in the summertime?" Pops asked. Jimmy is a truck driver, and he said soup was a favorite on the road because it's so portable and so filling.

I like making soup because it's a means to use any number of ingredients in an inventive way. (I like making cookies for the same reason.) You can let your creativity run wild, and the more outrageous you get, the more people like the outcome, as I discovered with the Spicy Cheeseburger Soup on page 57. My customers were wild for it.

In this chapter, I have taken some of the most basic soups in the American culinary lexicon—think tomato and mushroom soups—and funked them out. I have cream soups, broth soups, hearty soups, and vegetable soups on these pages. A few, such as the Loaded Baked Potato Soup (page 54) and the Spicy Cheeseburger Soup, could be substantial main courses. The others are great anytime, whether before a larger meal or as a light lunch or supper.

I have to confess, though: If you were to put a bowl of soup on the table next to a platter of wings, I'd go for the wings!

RECIPES

CREAM OF TOMATO AND RICE SOUP

Serves 6

- 3/4 cup white rice
- 3 cups canned diced tomatoes and their juice
- 1/2 cup (1 stick) unsalted butter
- 1/2 cup finely diced onion
- 1 tablespoon Italian Herb Blend (page 193)
- 1 teaspoon freshly ground black pepper
- 1/2 cup all-purpose flour
- 1 quart chicken broth
- 2 tablespoons chicken bouillon powder
- 1 cup heavy cream

TO PREPARE: Cook the rice according to the package directions. You should have about 1½ cups of cooked rice.

In a blender or food processor fitted with the metal blade, puree 1 cup of the tomatoes until smooth. Set aside.

In a large stockpot, melt the butter over medium-high heat. When hot, add the onion, herb blend, and pepper and cook, stirring, until the onion softens, 4 to 5 minutes.

Stir the flour into the onion to create a thick mixture and cook, stirring, for 3 to 5 minutes. Add the broth, bouillon powder, the remaining 2 cups of tomatoes, and the pureed tomatoes. Cook, stirring occasionally, until the soup thickens slightly, 10 to 15 minutes.

Stir the cooked rice and heavy cream into the soup. When heated through, remove from the heat and let the soup rest for about 5 minutes before serving.

LOADED BAKED POTATO SOUP

Serves 8

3 cups peeled, diced potatoes (about 3 medium baking potatoes)
1½ cups canola oil
½ cup finely diced celery
½ cup finely diced onion
1 tablespoon chopped garlic
1 tablespoon freshly ground black pepper
1 teaspoon dried thyme
1 cup all-purpose flour
1 quart chicken broth
3 tablespoons chicken bouillon powder
2 cups heavy cream
8 ounces sliced bacon, cooked until crispy and crumbled (about ½ cup)
2 cups shredded cheddar cheese
½ cup chopped scallions, white and green parts

TO PREPARE: In a large saucepan, put the potatoes and enough water to cover them by about 2 inches. Bring to a boil over high heat. Lower the heat to medium and simmer, uncovered, until fork-tender, about 15 minutes. Drain and return to the pan. Cover and keep warm.

In a large stockpot, heat the oil over medium-high heat. When hot, add the celery, onion, garlic, pepper, and thyme and cook, stirring, until the vegetables soften, 6 to 8 minutes. Add in the flour to create a thick mixture and cook, stirring, for 3 to 5 minutes. Add the broth, bouillon powder, and potatoes and cook, stirring, for 10 to 15 minutes.

Stir in the heavy cream and bacon, bring to a simmer, and cook until heated through and the flavors meld, about 20 minutes, stirring occasionally. Remove the soup from the heat, add the cheese and scallions, stir well to incorporate both into the soup, and serve.

SPICY CHEESEBURGER SOUP

Serves 12

1 cup peeled, diced potato (1 medium all-purpose potato)
½ cup canola oil
2 pounds ground beef
1 cup finely diced onion
½ cup diced green bell pepper
½ cup diced red bell pepper
½ cup diced jalapeño chile peppers
1 cup all-purpose flour
1 tablespoon Italian Herb Blend (page 193)
1 tablespoon kosher salt
1 tablespoon freshly ground black pepper
1½ quarts beef broth
¼ cup beef bouillon powder
1½ pounds white American cheese, thickly sliced
¼ cup chopped scallions, white and green parts

TO PREPARE: In a large saucepan, put the potatoes and enough water to cover them by about 2 inches. Bring to a boil over high heat. Lower the heat to medium and simmer, uncovered, until fork-tender, about 15 minutes. Drain and return to the pan. Cover and keep warm.

In a large stockpot, heat the oil over medium-high heat. When hot, add the beef and cook, breaking up the meat slightly with a wooden spoon, until the beef begins to brown, 6 to 10 minutes. Add the onion and bell peppers and cook, stirring, for another minute or two. Add the jalapeños and then the flour, herb blend, salt, and black pepper. Cook, stirring, until well mixed and thickened, 3 to 4 minutes.

Add the broth and bouillon powder, lower the heat to medium, and cook, stirring, until heated through, taking care not to break the meat up too much.

Remove the pan from the heat, add the slices of cheese, one at a time, and stir gently until the cheese melts into the soup and the soup becomes creamy. Add the scallions and potatoes and cook just until heated through. Serve hot.

WHAT IS THE BEST WAY TO COOK BACON?

I love bacon. Even I can't improve on its intrinsic deliciousness. I like to grill it, but I understand that it's not always feasible to fire up the grill for a few slices of bacon, so I will explain how I grill bacon and also how I cook it in the oven.

When you grill bacon, begin with thick-cut slices. I like to buy a slab and slice it myself or buy it from a butcher who slices it according to how I want it, but there is some very good precut thick bacon in supermarkets, too.

You can grill the bacon directly on the rack or spread it on a baking sheet. If you want to put it directly on the grill rack, put a drip pan under the rack to catch the bacon fat and position the bacon away from the coals (indirect cooking) or on a gas grill turned to medium. Close the lid while the bacon cooks—and keep a fire extinguisher or water bottle handy to deal with flare-ups. I like to add some mesquite or hickory chips to the fire to make the bacon taste even more intense.

I also bake bacon in the oven. I spread the slices on a baking sheet and cook them in a 400°F oven for 18 to 20 minutes. Watch it carefully and remove it when it reaches the desired degree of crispness. You don't have to turn the bacon as it bakes, but you do have to drain it on paper towels when you take it out of the oven. The oven is a good place to reheat bacon, too. Preheat the oven to 300°F and let the bacon heat for 4 to 7 minutes.

If you have leftover bacon—I know, hard to imagine!—or if you overcook it so that it's brittle, crumble it and add it to dips or creamy salad dressings. I also save the bacon fat and use it to add flavor to sautéed onions, mushrooms, and peppers—or just about anything!

LENTIL, PARSNIP, AND ROAST CORN SOUP

Serves 8 to 10

10 slices bacon
1 pound yellow lentils
1 cup finely chopped onion
1 cup finely chopped celery
2 heaping tablespoons chopped parsnips
2 quarts chicken broth
2 tablespoons chicken bouillon powder
½ teaspoon freshly ground black pepper
½ tablespoon Italian Herb Blend (page 193)
2 ears corn, husks and silks removed, or 1 to 1½ cups thawed frozen corn kernels
2 cups heavy cream
Crostini (small toasted bread slices from a baguette), for serving, optional

TO PREPARE: In a large skillet, cook the bacon over medium heat until crispy. Remove the bacon from the skillet and drain on paper towels. When cool enough to handle, crumble the bacon. Reserve the bacon fat in the skillet.

Measure ¼ cup of the reserved bacon fat and put it into a large stockpot. Heat over medium-high heat and, when hot, add the lentils, onion, celery, and parsnips. Cook, stirring, until the onion turns light brown, 4 to 5 minutes. Add the broth, bouillon powder, pepper, and Italian herb blend and bring to a simmer. Cook over medium heat, stirring frequently, until the vegetables are tender, 30 to 45 minutes.

Meanwhile, preheat the broiler.

Broil the ears of corn, turning several times, until lightly charred on all sides, 5 to 7 minutes. (Alternatively, spread the corn kernels in a shallow baking pan and broil for 5 to 7 minutes, stirring, until lightly charred.) When the ears of corn are cool enough to handle, slice the kernels from the cobs. Add the corn, bacon, and heavy cream to the soup, lower the heat to medium, and simmer gently until heated through, 10 to 12 minutes. Serve with the crostini, if desired.

CREAM OF WILD MUSHROOM SOUP WITH ROSEMARY

Serves 6

- ½ cup (1 stick) unsalted butter
- ¼ cup canola oil
- 1 cup sliced shiitake mushrooms
- 1 cup sliced cremini mushrooms
- 1 cup sliced oyster mushrooms
- 1 cup sliced morel mushrooms
- 1 tablespoon chopped garlic
- 2 tablespoons fresh rosemary leaves
- 1 tablespoon chopped fresh thyme leaves
- ½ teaspoon freshly ground black pepper
- ½ cup all-purpose flour
- 1½ quarts chicken broth
- 2 tablespoons beef or chicken bouillon powder
- 1 cup heavy cream
- 2 tablespoons chopped fresh flat-leaf parsley

TO PREPARE: In a large pot, heat the butter and oil over medium-high heat until the butter melts and the mixture is hot and bubbling. Add the mushrooms, garlic, rosemary, thyme, and pepper and cook, stirring, until softened, 4 to 5 minutes. Sprinkle the flour over the mushrooms and stir until the flour blends with the pan liquids to form a smooth roux, 3 to 4 minutes.

Add the broth and bouillon powder to the pot and whisk until smooth. Lower the heat to medium and whisk in the heavy cream. Let the soup cook for a few minutes, until hot. Stir in the parsley and serve.

TOMATO AND FENNEL SOUP

Serves 4 to 6

1 tablespoon unsalted butter
2 tablespoons olive oil
1 fennel bulb, trimmed and sliced (about 2 cups)
2 tablespoons chopped garlic
2 teaspoons chopped fresh thyme leaves
One 15-ounce can peeled tomatoes, drained and diced
1½ quarts chicken broth
1 tablespoon fresh lemon juice
2 teaspoons salt
1 teaspoon freshly ground black pepper

TO PREPARE: In a large stockpot, heat the butter and oil over medium-high heat until the butter melts and the mixture is hot and bubbling. Add the fennel, garlic, and thyme and cook, stirring, until the fennel softens, about 4 minutes.

Add the tomatoes, broth, and lemon juice, and bring to a boil. Season with the salt and pepper and serve.

SIDE SALADS & BIGGER SALADS

I LIKE SALADS AS MUCH AS THE NEXT GUY—which means they have not always ranked high on my list of choice foods. But over the years, I have learned to sing a different tune about them and have created some rockin' recipes, if I do say so myself.

There's nothing fussy or dainty about my salads. Like the rest of my food, they erupt with flavor, texture, and color. Some are best served alongside another dish, such as the Summer Grapefruit Salad with Spicy Walnuts and Honey-Mint Dressing (page 76) and the Honeydew and Prosciutto Salad with Fresh Herbs (page 78). My Spicy Beef Salad with Peppers, Onion, and Fresh Herbs (page 80) is without question a main course, as is the Hoagie Salad (page 67).

My wife, Kim, loves salads, and I have to dedicate this chapter to her. She inspired me to rethink my attitude and come up with some of the best dishes in my arsenal. These salads are unequaled in the world of relatively light dishes meant to be served cold or at room temperature. Try them. You'll see!

RECIPES

HOAGIE SALAD

When my new neighbor Colleen discovered I had a television show on the Food Network, she urged me to try her hoagie salad. She thought my viewers might like it. I am a Jersey boy, through and through, and so naturally I am a major fan of hoagies, those packed-full sandwiches people in other parts of the country call subs or grinders. We have the best hoagies in New Jersey, hands down. There's no competition, and this hoagie salad duplicates the flavors perfectly. I funked it out a little, because that's the way I cook, but I dedicate this recipe to Colleen and thank her for sharing it with me.

Serves 4 to 6

1½ cups mayonnaise
½ cup chopped scallions, white and green parts
¼ cup seeded and chopped cherry peppers
2 tablespoons Worcestershire sauce
1 tablespoon chopped fresh oregano
1 tablespoon freshly ground black pepper
½ cup diced capicola (also called coppa; a generous 4 ounces)
½ cup diced Genoa salami (a generous 4 ounces)
½ cup diced pepperoni (a generous 4 ounces)
½ cup diced ham (a generous 4 ounces)
½ cup diced provolone cheese (a generous 4 ounces)
2 cups torn arugula leaves
One 16- to 18-inch-long Italian baguette
1½ cups halved cherry tomatoes

TO PREPARE: In a large bowl, mix together the mayonnaise, scallions, cherry peppers, Worcestershire sauce, oregano, and black pepper. Add the diced meats, cheese, and arugula and fold to mix well.

Cut the baguette into 1-inch-wide pieces and serve alongside the salad. Top the salad with the tomatoes.

BACON AND PESTO PASTA SALAD

I used to cater from my restaurant several years ago, and when Rutgers University in Camden asked for some salads for a catering gig, I came up with this one. It's loosely based on a turkey wrap I made for the restaurant, although there is no wrap in sight here. The longer this salad sits, the better it tastes, so this is a good one to make ahead of time.

Serves 6 to 8

- 1 pound rotini
- 8 slices bacon, cooked until crispy and crumbled
- 1 cup shredded parmesan cheese, plus more for garnish
- 1 cup roasted red pepper strips (two 4-ounce jars)
- ½ cup thinly sliced red onion
- ½ cup oil-packed sun-dried tomatoes
- 1 cup packed fresh basil leaves
- ¼ cup fresh lemon juice (3 to 4 lemons)
- 2 tablespoons chopped garlic
- 2 tablespoons kosher salt
- 1 tablespoon freshly ground black pepper
- 1 cup olive oil

TO PREPARE: In a medium saucepan, cook the pasta according to the package directions until al dente. Drain (but do not rinse) and transfer to a dish to cool to room temperature. The pasta can be chilled until ready to use.

In a large bowl, toss the pasta with the bacon, parmesan, roasted pepper strips, onion, and sun-dried tomatoes.

In a food processor fitted with the metal blade, pulse the basil with the lemon juice, garlic, salt, and black pepper until well mixed. With the processor running, slowly drizzle the olive oil through the feed tube into the pesto and pulse until smooth. Spoon the pesto over the pasta mixture and toss until evenly coated.

Cover and refrigerate for at least 1 hour and up to 3 hours to give the flavors time to blend. Serve chilled or at room temperature, garnished with parmesan.

ULTIMATE CHICKEN SALAD AND ULTIMATE TUNA SALAD

I once had a job setting up the buffet at the now-closed Harbor League Club in Camden, New Jersey. One day the members surprised me with a plaque that read "Best Chicken Salad Ever." This is the first time I have shared my recipe, and I hope when you make it you get a plaque, too! Both the chicken and the tuna salad recipes that follow are best when well mixed. I usually use my hands, so don't be shy about digging in.

BOTH RECIPES ARE BEST WHEN WELL MIXED. I USUALLY USE MY HANDS, SO DON'T BE SHY ABOUT DIGGING IN.

ULTIMATE CHICKEN SALAD

Serves 8 to 10; makes about 7 cups

6 cups chopped or shredded cooked chicken breast meat (3 to 5 boneless whole breasts; 1½ to 2 pounds total)
1½ cups mayonnaise
¼ cup finely diced onion
¼ cup finely diced celery
¼ cup sweet pickle relish
1 bunch (about 1 ounce) fresh chives, chopped
2 tablespoons Worcestershire sauce
1 tablespoon kosher salt
1 tablespoon hot pepper sauce, such as Tabasco
1 teaspoon freshly ground black pepper

TO PREPARE: In a large bowl, toss the chicken with the mayonnaise, onion, celery, relish, chives, Worcestershire sauce, salt, hot pepper sauce, and black pepper. Cover and refrigerate for at least 1 hour and up to 2 days.

ULTIMATE TUNA SALAD

Serves 6 to 8; makes about 4 cups

Three 6-ounce cans water-packed albacore tuna, well drained
1 cup mayonnaise
⅓ cup finely diced onion
⅓ cup finely diced celery
2 tablespoons sweet pickle relish
2 tablespoons Worcestershire sauce
2 teaspoons kosher salt
2 teaspoons hot pepper sauce, such as Tabasco
1 teaspoon freshly ground black pepper

TO PREPARE: In a large bowl, toss the tuna with the mayonnaise, onion, celery, relish, Worcestershire sauce, salt, hot pepper sauce, and black pepper. Cover and refrigerate for at least 1 hour and up to 2 days.

FAMILY-STYLE CURRY CHICKEN SALAD PLATTER

My niece Tori used to help me out in the restaurant, particularly when I was catering a big party. She loved my chicken curry and usually asked for it with a little fruit on the side. I decided to add a chicken curry platter to the menu, and it was an immediate hit, particularly in the summertime. Your family will like it, too.

Serves 4 to 6 as a main dish, 8 to 10 as a side salad

- 2 cups Ultimate Chicken Salad (page 71)
- 1½ cups green grapes
- ½ cup chopped scallions, white and green parts
- ½ cup mayonnaise
- 2 tablespoons mild or hot curry powder
- 4 cups mesclun salad mix or two 10-ounce bags
- 2 cups cubed fresh pineapple
- 2 cups cubed ripe cantaloupe
- 2 cups cubed ripe honeydew
- 1 pint grape tomatoes
- 1 cup cucumber slices

TO PREPARE: In a large bowl, mix the chicken salad with the grapes, scallions, mayonnaise, and curry powder.

In the center of a large platter, arrange the mesclun to create a bed for the chicken salad. Spoon the chicken salad over the greens and top with the pineapple, cantaloupe, honeydew, grape tomatoes, and cucumber slices. Serve immediately.

MEDITERRANEAN AHI TUNA PASTA SALAD

Ahi tuna is delicious and tender—and expensive. But you don't need a lot of it to make a big impression, as this salad demonstrates. I think the salad showcases ahi to its best advantage with a Mediterranean flair. It's an amazing picnic dish, needing nothing more than a crusty roll and a glass of wine.

Serves 6

½ cup plus 2 tablespoons olive oil
¾ cup sliced black and green olives
¼ cup red wine vinegar
¼ cup drained and sliced pepperoncini
¼ cup sliced scallions, white and green parts
2 tablespoons chopped fresh cilantro
1 teaspoon crushed red pepper flakes
1 teaspoon freshly cracked black pepper
Six 4-ounce fillets ahi tuna
Salt and freshly ground black pepper
1 pound spaghetti (I use #9 spaghetti, which is thick)
½ cup julienned jarred roasted red peppers
¼ cup thinly sliced red onion
¼ cup capers, drained
1¼ cups coarsely crumbled feta cheese
1 cup coarsely chopped and drained marinated artichoke hearts

TO PREPARE: In a large bowl, toss ½ cup of the olive oil with the olives, vinegar, pepperoncini, scallions, cilantro, red pepper flakes, and cracked black pepper. Set aside to marinate.

In a large skillet, heat the remaining 2 tablespoons of olive oil over medium-high heat. When hot, lightly season the tuna fillets with salt and pepper and sear until lightly crusted, 2 to 3 minutes on each side. Lift the tuna from the pan, transfer to a dish, and refrigerate for 20 to 30 minutes, until chilled.

Meanwhile, cook the spaghetti according to the package directions until al dente. Drain but do not rinse. Let the pasta cool to room temperature.

Add the spaghetti to the bowl with the olives and pepperoncini and toss until the pasta is nicely coated. Transfer to a serving platter. Cut the chilled tuna on the bias into ½-inch-thick slices and shingle these over the pasta. Sprinkle with the roasted peppers, onion, and capers, and then top with the feta. Garnish with the artichoke hearts and serve.

WHAT IS THE BEST WAY TO COOK PASTA?

I like to cook pasta until it's al dente, which means it is still a little firm. The term means "to the tooth" and refers to how properly cooked pasta has a pleasant little bite to it.

To cook pasta so that it's perfect every time, use a large pot (I usually use a stockpot) and measure a gallon of water for every pound of pasta. Add a teaspoon of salt to the water for every pound of pasta—I use sea salt or kosher salt. When the water boils over high heat, add the pasta. Don't break the pasta; put it in the water as it comes from the package and let it sink into the pot.

Keep the pot over high heat, and when the water returns to a boil, gently stir the pasta. I stir it with a large wooden spoon pretty much constantly for 12 to 15 minutes until it's done. Some pastas may take a little more time and others a little less.

Drain the pasta and set it aside or use as you want. Don't rinse it! That only washes away flavor and prevents any sauce from properly adhering to the pasta.

SUMMER GRAPEFRUIT SALAD WITH SPICY WALNUTS AND HONEY-MINT DRESSING

This is one of the best summer salads going. The fruit pops in the mouth, the nuts crunch, and the honey and mint add sweetness and interest. It's super-light and super-refreshing, and if you add some grilled chicken, you have a meal. I came up with this salad when my sister Carla stopped by with some grapefruit one day, but if you don't feel like peeling and sectioning the fruit, buy the grapefruit already sectioned.

Serves 6

SPICY WALNUTS:

1 cup sugar
1 cup walnut halves
1 teaspoon cayenne pepper
1 teaspoon salt
½ teaspoon paprika

HONEY-MINT DRESSING:

½ cup fresh lime juice
¾ cup canola oil
¼ cup olive oil
2 tablespoons diced shallots
2 tablespoons chopped fresh mint leaves
2 teaspoons honey
1 tablespoon grated lime zest
1 tablespoon kosher salt
1 teaspoon freshly ground black pepper

SALAD:

2 cups spring greens salad mix
1 bulb fennel, trimmed and thinly sliced
1 cup dried cranberries
2 grapefruits, peeled and cut into sections
1 cup crumbled goat cheese

TO MAKE THE WALNUTS: Preheat the oven to 300°F. Line a baking sheet with parchment paper.

In a small saucepan, bring ½ cup of water and the sugar to a boil over high heat and stir until the sugar dissolves. Add the walnuts to the syrup and cook, stirring frequently, for about 2 minutes. Drain the walnuts and transfer them to a medium bowl.

Sprinkle the nuts with the cayenne, salt, and paprika and toss well. Spread the walnuts on the prepared baking sheet and bake, stirring once or twice, for 14 to 16 minutes, until the walnuts deepen a shade or two and are fragrant. Slide the walnuts onto a plate to cool.

TO MAKE THE DRESSING: Put the lime juice in the blender and with the machine running, slowly drizzle the canola oil into the canister. When the canola oil is added, add the olive oil in the same slow manner, increasing the speed toward the end of blending.

Add the shallots, mint, honey, lime zest, salt, and pepper and pulse for about 2 minutes, or until incorporated and blended. There will be visible pieces of mint and lime zest in the dressing, which is fine.

TO MAKE THE SALAD: In a large serving bowl, toss the greens with the fennel, cranberries and dressing. Top with the grapefruit sections, goat cheese, and walnuts. Serve immediately.

IT'S SUPER-LIGHT AND SUPER-REFRESHING, AND IF YOU ADD SOME GRILLED CHICKEN, YOU HAVE A MEAL.

HONEYDEW AND PROSCIUTTO SALAD WITH FRESH HERBS

This salad is something of a sleeper. You may not be tempted to make it, but I urge you to try it because when you do, your taste buds will wake up! Make this recipe when honeydew is at its sweetest and juiciest, and you will have a top-notch salad. I was inspired by melon wrapped in prosciutto, but I like this salad even more than that. It's totally refreshing and very pretty, too.

Serves 6 to 8

- ½ cup sugar
- 2 honeydew melons, seeded, peeled, and diced
- 1 teaspoon cayenne pepper
- Pinch of salt
- Pinch of freshly cracked black pepper
- 8 ounces prosciutto, finely chopped
- ¼ cup fresh tarragon leaves
- ¼ cup finely sliced fresh basil leaves
- ¼ cup finely sliced fresh flat-leaf parsley leaves

TO PREPARE: In a small saucepan, bring ¼ cup of water and the sugar to a boil over high heat and stir until the sugar dissolves. When the syrup is clear, pour it into a small metal bowl. Set the small bowl in a larger bowl filled with ice and cold water to cool down the syrup.

In a large bowl, season the melon with the cayenne, salt, and pepper. Add the prosciutto, tarragon, basil, and parsley and toss lightly. Pour the syrup over the salad, mix well, transfer to a serving platter, and serve.

HOW CAN I TELL IF A MELON IS RIPE?

Most muskmelons, which include cantaloupe, honeydew, and Crenshaw, are easy to find in the markets all year long, but too often we're disappointed when we cut into them because they are hard and tasteless. It's important to let them ripen on the countertop before using them. A ripe melon will have a discernible fragrance, particularly the summer melons (those with wrinkly skin; think cantaloupe). The stem end will feel a little soft when you press on it and the melon will feel heavy. When you buy melons, choose those that are free of blemishes or shriveled skin. And try to select a ripe one so that you can enjoy it right away!

A RIPE MELON WILL HAVE A DISCERNIBLE FRAGRANCE, PARTICULARY THE SUMMER MELONS (THOSE WITH THE WRINKLY SKIN; THINK CANTALOUPE).

SPICY BEEF SALAD WITH PEPPERS, ONION, AND FRESH HERBS

Beef salads are terrific any time of year, but I especially like them in the summer, when it's easy to grill the steak. This salad is pretty intense and spicy and pops with color and flavor. The dressing is unusual and, while it's spicy, I mellow it out with the orange juice and sugar.

Serves 4 to 6

VINAIGRETTE:

¼ cup orange juice
¼ cup soy sauce
¼ cup Sriracha or another hot pepper sauce
2 tablespoons olive oil
Pinch of sugar

STEAK:

6 chipotle chile peppers in adobo sauce
½ cup olive oil
Juice of 2 limes
Salt and freshly ground black pepper
1¼ pounds flank steak

SALAD:

4 whole roasted jarred red peppers, cut into strips
2 jalapeño chile peppers, seeded and thinly sliced
1 bunch fresh cilantro leaves, chopped
1 medium red onion, thinly sliced
1 cup salted peanuts
½ cup freshly shucked corn kernels or thawed frozen kernels
Two 10-ounce bags mesclun salad mix, or one 10-ounce bag mesclun salad mix and one 11½-ounce bag baby spinach

recipe continued on page 82

TO MAKE THE VINAIGRETTE: In a small glass, ceramic, or another nonreactive bowl, whisk together the orange juice, soy sauce, Sriracha, and olive oil. Season to taste with sugar and set aside.

TO MAKE THE STEAK: In a blender, puree the chipotle peppers, olive oil, lime juice, and salt and black pepper to taste to a thick paste. Rub the paste over both sides of the flank steak and put the steak in a glass dish. Set aside at room temperature for 30 to 60 minutes. (Do not leave the steak at room temperature for longer than 60 minutes.)

Meanwhile, prepare a medium-hot to hot fire in a charcoal or gas grill and oil the grill grates. Grill for 6 to 7 minutes on each side, until medium-rare. Transfer to a cutting board, let the steak rest for about 5 minutes, and slice on the bias into thin slices.

TO MAKE THE SALAD: In a large glass, ceramic, or another nonreactive bowl, toss together the roasted peppers, jalapeños, cilantro, red onion, peanuts, and corn. Dress with the vinaigrette, reserving a few tablespoons to dress the steak. Arrange the greens on a serving platter and top with the peanut-corn mixture. Shingle the steak over the salad, drizzle with the remaining dressing, and serve.

BEEF SALADS ARE TERRIFIC ANY TIME OF YEAR, BUT I ESPECIALLY LIKE THEM IN THE SUMMER, WHEN IT'S EASY TO GRILL THE STEAK.

SANDWICHES THAT BURST WITH FLAVOR

I HAVE ALWAYS UNDERSTOOD SANDWICHES. In my opinion, nothing compares to gripping a couple pieces of bread filled with tempting, tasty food and lifting it to your mouth for a big, satisfying bite. Some of the mayo or cheese may drip down your chin, and you probably will have to grab some napkins before the next bite, but man-oh-man: that sandwich is good!

I had a hard time keeping the number of sandwiches in the book to a manageable number. I am pretty sure I could come up with ideas for these gastronomic treats for days on end and never duplicate a single one. I like to renew old standards, invent new combinations, and embellish on others that barely need improving (but that never stopped me!).

Whether you are looking for a big, hearty sandwich or lighter fare, you will find something here to satisfy your hunger. Try the Pastrami and Frizzled Fried Onion Sandwiches (page 101) or the Grilled Bratwurst Hoagies with Creamy Coleslaw (page 88) for oversized sandwiches. Think about the Grilled Marinated Portobello Mushroom Sandwiches (page 110) or the Jerk Chicken Sandwiches with Smoked Gouda (page 97) for something slightly less intense. I promise: when you are in the mood for a good sandwich, you will find something to meet your expectations right here.

RECIPES

TURKEY BURGERS WITH GRILLED PEPPERS AND ONION AND SMOKED CHEDDAR

When Kimberly and I first started dating, she told me she made a mean turkey burger. I had never had a turkey burger in my life, and while her burger was okay, it was, well… it was just a turkey burger on a bun. I dressed it up a little with smoked cheddar and grilled peppers and onion and mixed the ground turkey with ranch dressing for flavor and moisture. Kim loves my version, which is one of the most popular offerings in our house.

Serves 4

- ½ medium red bell pepper, halved and seeded
- ½ medium yellow bell pepper, halved and seeded
- 2 jalapeño chile peppers, halved and seeded
- 1 medium sweet onion, such as Vidalia, sliced into ¼-inch-thick disks
- 2 tablespoons olive oil, plus more, for drizzling
- Salt and freshly cracked black pepper
- ½ cup Arugula Mayonnaise (page 181)
- 4 round Portuguese rolls, split
- 1½ pounds ground turkey
- 1 envelope dry ranch dressing mix (about 2 tablespoons)
- 4 slices smoked cheddar cheese

TO PREPARE: Prepare a hot fire in a charcoal or gas grill and oil the grill grates.

Toss the bell peppers, jalapeños, and onion slices with 2 tablespoons of the olive oil and season with salt and black pepper. Grill for 3 to 4 minutes on each side, until the outside of the peppers and the onion are nicely charred—not burned—and the vegetables begin to soften. Remove the peppers and onion from the grill and set aside to cool slightly. When cool enough to handle, slice the peppers into strips and toss with the onion.

Spread the mayonnaise on the rolls and set aside.

In a large bowl, mix the ground turkey with the ranch dressing mix. Form the meat into 4 patties and put on a platter lined with parchment paper. Drizzle olive oil over the burgers and season lightly with salt and black pepper. Grill for 4 to 5 minutes on each side, until the burgers are just cooked through. Top each burger with a slice of cheese and cook for an additional minute, until the cheese melts. Put a burger between the halves of the rolls, top with the peppers and onions, and serve.

GRILLED BRATWURST HOAGIES WITH CREAMY COLESLAW

I remember watching a television show once about tailgating recipes during which everyone cooked bratwurst with peppers and onions. While this is a good way to eat brats, I decided to make a brat hoagie with cool, creamy coleslaw instead. The coleslaw can also stand on its own as a side or be served with other sandwiches. My brat sandwich is terrific for tailgating, by the way.

Serves 4

½ cup mayonnaise
½ cup sugar
¼ cup sour cream
¼ cup apple cider
2 tablespoons chopped fresh chives
Juice of 1 lemon
1 teaspoon cayenne pepper
Salt and freshly cracked black pepper
¼ head red cabbage, thinly sliced
¼ head green cabbage, thinly sliced
4 bratwurst sausages
4 steak or hoagie rolls, 8 to 10 inches long each, split

TO PREPARE: Prepare a hot fire in a charcoal or gas grill and oil the grill grates, or heat a countertop grill.

In a small bowl, stir together the mayonnaise, sugar, sour cream, cider, chives, lemon juice, and cayenne. Season to taste with salt and pepper. In a large bowl, toss the cabbages with the dressing. Use right away or cover and refrigerate for up to 8 hours.

Grill the bratwurst, turning frequently, for 8 to 10 minutes, until cooked through and browned. Put some coleslaw in each roll and top with a bratwurst. Top with a little more cabbage, if desired, and serve.

HOW DO I SHRED CABBAGE FOR COLESLAW?

It's easy to turn a head of red or green cabbage into shreds for coleslaw, and you will be amazed by how much roughage is in a typical head (which weighs about 2 pounds on average). Remove the outer leaves if they appear a little worn or wilted, and cut out the tough core. Cut the cabbage into large slices, and then cut them crosswise with a large, sharp knife to turn them into shreds. The thinner you slice them, the finer the shreds. For even thinner strands of cabbage, feed them through the shredding blade of the food processor.

CUT THE CABBAGE INTO LARGE SLICES, AND THEN CUT THEM CROSSWISE WITH A LARGE, SHARP KNIFE TO TURN THEM INTO SHREDS.

MARINATED CHICKEN CLUBS WITH PESTO MAYONNAISE AND SUN-DRIED TOMATOES

Everyone likes turkey clubs, but let's face it: they are a little old-school. I decided to funk out a club sandwich by making it with chicken and delicious pesto mayonnaise to bump up the flavor a little. The tomatoes are a little work but well worth it. I love the layers of flavor in this sandwich.

Serves 6

CHICKEN:

½ cup olive oil
2 tablespoons red wine vinegar
2 tablespoons fresh lemon juice
1 tablespoon chopped garlic
1 tablespoon chopped fresh oregano
1 teaspoon paprika
1 teaspoon ground cumin
1 teaspoon salt
1 teaspoon freshly ground black pepper
6 boneless, skinless chicken breast halves, each about 6 ounces, lightly pounded for even thickness

SANDWICHES:

12 slices Texas toast or another thick white sandwich bread, lightly toasted
1 cup Pesto Mayonnaise (page 186)
12 leaves Boston lettuce
6 large slices pepperoni
12 slices tomato
½ cup Marinated Sun-Dried Tomatoes (page 197), coarsely chopped
12 slices cooked bacon
6 slices provolone cheese

recipe continued on page 92

TO PREPARE THE CHICKEN: Line a baking sheet or shallow baking pan with parchment paper. In a small glass, ceramic, or another nonreactive bowl, stir together the olive oil, vinegar, lemon juice, garlic, oregano, paprika, cumin, salt, and black pepper. Rub or brush the chicken breasts with liberal amounts of the marinade mixture and transfer each breast to the prepared baking sheet. Cover with plastic wrap and refrigerate for about 30 minutes to marinate.

TO MAKE THE SANDWICHES: In a preheated countertop grill, grill the chicken until cooked through, 4 to 6 minutes. (Alternatively, cook the chicken in a lightly oiled large skillet set over medium-high heat for 2 to 4 minutes on each side.)

Top 6 slices of the bread with some of the mayonnaise, 2 lettuce leaves, 1 pepperoni slice, 2 tomato slices, sun-dried tomatoes, 2 bacon slices, and 1 cheese slice. Add a chicken breast half to each sandwich. Spread the remaining 6 slices of bread with more mayonnaise and top the sandwiches. Press gently to close the sandwiches and serve.

I DECIDED TO FUNK OUT A CLUB SANDWICH BY MAKING IT WITH CHICKEN AND DELICIOUS PESTO MAYONNAISE TO BUMP UP THE FLAVOR A LITTLE.

INSIDE-OUT PULLED PORK PANINI WITH ARUGULA AND CHIPOTLE MAYONNAISE

When you are making this sandwich, you might want to roll up your sleeves—it's pretty messy! Don't let the instructions scare you. Read them carefully and slowly and then go for it. It will make sense to build the sandwich with the rolls turned upside down—you won't be disappointed. You'll love it! I came up with this sandwich after I had made the Cuban Sandwiches on page 109 and had some leftover pulled pork. The sandwich is crunchy and peppery, with the arugula giving it one kind of peppery-ness and the chipotle mayonnaise another.

Serves 4

- 4 ciabatta rolls or 8 thick slices ciabatta bread
- 1/4 cup Chipotle Mayonnaise (page 185)
- About 3 cups Pulled Pork (page 94)
- 1/4 cup Pulled Pork cooking sauce (page 95)
- Eight 1/4-inch-thick slices sharp cheddar cheese (I like Cooper)
- 2 cups baby arugula leaves
- 2 tablespoons unsalted butter, softened

TO PREPARE: Separate the rolls so that you have 8 halves. Spread the mayonnaise on the outside, crusty side of each roll. Lay the 4 bottom halves of the rolls, mayonnaise side up, on a work surface.

In a large bowl, stir the pulled pork with the cooking sauce.

Spoon equal amounts of the pork over the 4 bottom halves of the rolls. Add 2 cheese slices to each half. Put the arugula on top of the cheese and then top each sandwich with the remaining roll halves, so that the mayonnaise-spread sides are facing down. Press down gently on the sandwiches.

Spread the butter over both sides of each sandwich. Because the sandwich is "inside-out," you will be spreading the butter on the traditional inside of the rolls. Cut each sandwich in half and put the sandwiches in a heated panini press. Close the press and cook for 5 to 6 minutes, until the sandwiches are toasty and warmed through. (Alternatively, melt about 1½ tablespoons of unsalted butter in a 12-inch nonstick skillet over medium-high heat. When the butter melts, put the sandwiches in the pan, top with a weight or a small skillet, lower the heat to medium, and cook for 5 to 6 minutes on each side, until the filling is hot.) Serve hot.

PULLED PORK

You may not want to take the time to cook the pork, but once you do, you can freeze what you don't use and then have it on hand for Cuban Sandwiches (page 109) or Inside-Out Pulled Pork Panini with Arugula and Chipotle Mayonnaise (page 93) any old time. It's not difficult to cook the pork; it just takes time. Do it on a day when you will be home and can let it braise very slowly in the oven.

Makes 5 to 6 cups

3 tablespoons kosher salt
2 tablespoons coarsely ground black pepper
2 tablespoons smoked paprika
1 tablespoon granulated garlic powder
3 pounds boneless pork shoulder
3 tablespoons canola or grapeseed oil
1 medium onion, sliced
6 cloves garlic, smashed
2 jalapeño chile peppers, slit open with a knife
2 tablespoons tomato paste
2 cups beef broth
½ cup Worcestershire sauce

TO PREPARE: Preheat the oven to 325°F.

In a small bowl, mix together the salt, black pepper, paprika, and garlic powder. Rub the spice mixture into the pork shoulder, using all the spices and rubbing it into all sides. Set the pork aside for about 20 minutes to reach room temperature.

In a large Dutch oven or similar pot, heat the oil over medium-high heat. When hot, sear the pork shoulder until the meat is crusty and nicely browned on all sides, 5 to 6 minutes total. Lift the pork from the pot and set aside on a platter.

Add the onion, garlic, and jalapeños to the pot and cook, stirring, until the vegetables are nicely browned, about 5 minutes. Stir in the tomato paste and cook for about 2 minutes. Add the broth and Worcestershire sauce and bring to a simmer.

Return the pork to the pot, cover, and roast in the oven until the meat is fork-tender and nearly falling apart, 4 to 5 hours. Remove the pork from the pot and set aside to cool.

When the pork is cool enough to handle, shred the meat using your fingers or a fork, and put the meat in a bowl. Discard any fatty pieces. Cover and refrigerate until ready to use.

Strain the cooking juices from the pot through a sieve into another bowl. Refrigerate the juices for at least 1 hour, or until you can skim and discard the fat that rises to the top.

Spoon as much of the defatted cooking juices into the pulled pork as needed to moisten it; you will need at least ½ cup and perhaps more. If the meat appears moist, you may not need the juices. Refrigerate or freeze the unused juices separately from the meat. Moisten the meat as needed with the reserved juices. They can be refrigerated for up to 5 days and frozen for up to 1 month.

IT'S NOT DIFFICULT TO COOK THE PORK; IT JUST TAKES TIME. DO IT ON A DAY WHEN YOU WILL BE HOME AND CAN LET IT BRAISE VERY SLOWLY.

JERK CHICKEN SANDWICHES WITH SMOKED GOUDA

I have never seen another jerk chicken sandwich, but why not?

Serves 4

½ cup olive oil
2 tablespoons chopped fresh cilantro leaves
1 tablespoon chopped fresh thyme
2 to 3 jalapeño chile peppers
Juice of 2 limes
1 tablespoon freshly ground black pepper
2 teaspoons brown sugar
2 teaspoons kosher salt
1 teaspoon allspice
½ teaspoon freshly grated nutmeg
½ teaspoon ground cinnamon
½ cup Roasted Garlic Mayonnaise (page 179)
8 boneless, skinless chicken breast halves, pounded thin (see Note, page 117)
4 steak or hoagie rolls, 8 to 10 inches long each, split
8 thick slices smoked Gouda cheese
Red Peppadew peppers, for garnish, optional

TO PREPARE: In the bowl of a food processor fitted with the metal blade, mix together the olive oil, cilantro, thyme, jalapeños, lime juice, black pepper, sugar, salt, allspice, nutmeg, and cinnamon. Pulse the marinade until smooth. In a small bowl, stir ¼ cup of the marinade into the garlic mayonnaise. Cover and refrigerate until needed.

In a shallow ceramic or glass dish, add the chicken and pour the remaining marinade over it, turning to coat. Cover the dish and refrigerate for 2 to 6 hours.

Prepare a hot fire in a charcoal or gas grill and oil the grill grates.

Lift the chicken from the marinade, letting most of it drip off the meat. Grill for 3 to 4 minutes on each side, until cooked through and the meat develops a nice char. Put 2 cutlets side by side on bottom half of each roll and top with 2 slices of cheese to cover the chicken. Lower the heat on the gas grill or find a cool part of the charcoal grill. Put the bottom of the sandwich with the chicken and cheese back on the grill. Cover the grill and let the sandwiches grill for 2 to 3 minutes, until the cheese melts.

Spread each top of the roll with garlic mayonnaise. Garnished the sandwiches with Peppadew Peppers, if desired. Cover the sadwiches with the tops of the rolls and press gently. Serve hot.

BARBECUED BEEF WITH PICKLE SLAW ON TOASTED SOFT ROLLS

Here's another way to make good use of the Shredded Beef Short Ribs on page 24. This is a great summery sandwich, although I eat it all year long, and the pickle slaw is incredibly refreshing. When you eat this, you'll need a lot of napkins.

Serves 4 to 6

- 2½ pounds boneless beef short ribs
- 2 tablespoons kosher salt, plus more as needed
- 2 tablespoons coarsely ground black pepper, plus more as needed
- 3 tablespoons canola oil
- 1 medium onion, sliced
- 5 cloves garlic, smashed
- 1 cup ketchup
- ¾ cup beef broth
- 2 tablespoons cider vinegar
- 2 tablespoons fresh lemon juice
- 2 tablespoons Worcestershire sauce
- 2 tablespoons brown sugar
- 1 tablespoon smoked paprika
- 4 to 6 soft rolls, split
- Pickle Slaw (page 100)

TO PREPARE: Preheat the oven to 425°F. Season the short ribs generously with salt and pepper.

In a large Dutch oven or similar pot, heat the oil over medium-high heat. When hot, sear the short ribs on all sides until the meat is crusty and nicely browned, 5 to 6 minutes total. Lift the short ribs from the pot and set aside on a platter.

Add the onion and garlic to the pot and cook, stirring, until nicely browned, about 5 minutes. Stir in the ketchup, broth, vinegar, lemon juice, Worcestershire sauce, sugar, and paprika and bring to a simmer. Taste and season with salt and pepper.

Return the ribs to the pot, cover, and roast in the oven until the beef is fork-tender, about 2 hours. Remove the pot from the oven and set aside to allow the meat to cool.

When the ribs are cool enough to handle, lift them from the pot, shred the meat using your fingers or a fork, and put it in a bowl. You will have about 3 cups of shredded short ribs. Set aside until ready to use.

recipe continued on page 100

Strain the cooking juices through a sieve into another bowl. Refrigerate the juices until you can skim and discard the fat that rises to the top, 20 to 30 minutes.

Spoon as much of the defatted cooking juices into the rib meat as needed to moisten it. You will need at least ¼ cup and perhaps more.

Reheat the meat on high power in the microwave until heated through, 1 to 2 minutes.

Preheat the broiler and toast the rolls, cut sides up, for 1 to 2 minutes, until nicely browned.

Pile equal amounts of meat on the bottom half of each roll and top with pickle slaw. Put the top half of the roll on each sandwich, press gently, and serve.

PICKLE SLAW

Makes 3½ to 4 cups

- 1 cup thinly shredded green cabbage
- 1 cup thinly shredded red cabbage
- 1 cup julienned baby dill pickles
- ½ cup julienned carrots
- ⅓ cup thinly sliced red onion
- 2 jalapeño chile peppers, very thinly sliced
- ⅓ cup mayonnaise
- 1 tablespoon cider vinegar
- ½ teaspoon sugar
- ¼ teaspoon smoked or kosher salt
- ¼ teaspoon coarsely ground black pepper

TO PREPARE: In a large bowl, stir together the cabbages, pickles, carrots, onion, and jalapeños. In a small bowl, whisk together the mayonnaise, vinegar, sugar, salt, and black pepper.

Pour the dressing over the vegetables and toss until well mixed. Cover and refrigerate the slaw for at least 30 minutes to marinate.

PASTRAMI AND FRIZZLED FRIED ONION SANDWICHES

As any good pastrami sandwich should be, this is a hearty, filling one with tons of flavor. The first time I tasted pastrami, it was served hot on rye bread with mustard. I thought it deserved a little more attention, and so I added these splendid fried onions.

Serves 6

FRIED ONIONS:

1 quart canola oil
1 cup all-purpose flour
2 tablespoons Dig It Spice Blend (page 191)
3 cups thinly sliced onions (3 to 4 medium onions)
Salt, optional

SANDWICHES:

12 slices rye bread
1 cup Horseradish Mustard (page 188)
12 thick slices Swiss cheese
1½ pounds thinly sliced deli pastrami
About 1 cup (2 sticks) unsalted butter, melted

TO MAKE THE ONIONS: In a large, heavy pot, heat the oil over high heat until a deep-fat thermometer reaches a temperature of 350°F.

Put the flour in a shallow bowl and mix it with the spice blend. Coat the onion slices with the flour, shaking off any excess and separating the onion rings from each other. Using long-handled tongs or a slotted spoon, carefully submerge the onions, a few at a time so you don't crowd the pot, in the hot oil and fry, stirring with the tongs or spoon to ensure even frying, until very crispy, 2 to 3 minutes. Lift the onions from the oil with the tongs or slotted spoon and transfer to a large plate or baking sheet lined with paper towels to drain. Salt lightly, if desired. Let the oil return to 350°F between batches.

TO MAKE THE SANDWICHES: Spread 1 side of each piece of bread with the mustard and top 6 pieces of bread with 1 slice of cheese each and equal portions of the pastrami. Top with equal amounts of onions and another slice of cheese, and then top with bread.

Brush both sides of the sandwiches with the butter and put the sandwiches in a heated panini press or stovetop grill. You may not use all the butter, depending on your preferences, but bear in mind that the butter makes the bread brown and crispy. Close the press and cook until the sandwiches are toasty brown and warmed through, 3 to 4 minutes. (Alternatively, melt about 1½ tablespoons of unsalted butter in a 12-inch nonstick skillet over medium-high heat. When the butter melts, put the sandwiches in the pan, top with a weight or a small skillet, lower the heat to medium, and cook for 1 to 2 minutes on each side.) Serve hot.

PANINI WITH MEATBALLS AND MOZZARELLA CHEESE

If you are like me and can't get enough of meatball-parmesan sandwiches, you will love this. I always had trouble finding the right rolls for the sandwich. They either were too soft or too crispy, and so I decided to make this a panini, which, as it turned out, was a great idea! This is delicious and easy to eat. Panini bread is easy to find in supermarkets, and the meatballs and marinara are simple to make. Because the ingredients are homemade, this sandwich is super-good.

Serves 6

- 2 large eggs
- 1 cup dried Italian bread crumbs
- ¼ cup Worcestershire sauce
- One 1-ounce envelope onion soup mix
- 1 teaspoon granulated garlic powder
- 1 teaspoon crushed red pepper flakes
- 1 teaspoon salt
- 1 teaspoon freshly ground black pepper
- 2 pounds ground beef
- 6 panini flatbreads or large pita pockets
- 3 cups Easy Marinara Sauce (page 200)
- Twenty-four ⅛-inch-thick slices mozzarella cheese

TO PREPARE: Preheat the oven to 400°F.

In a large bowl, mix together the eggs, bread crumbs, Worcestershire sauce, onion soup mix, garlic powder, red pepper flakes, salt, and pepper. Add the ground beef and mix well.

With dampened palms, roll the meat mixture into 24 meatballs. Arrange the meatballs in a shallow baking pan and bake for about 20 minutes, or until cooked through. Remove from the oven and let the meatballs rest in the pan for about 15 minutes.

Split the breads in half but do not detach, so that they resemble clam shells. Put 2 slices of cheese on each sandwich. Split the meatballs in half and arrange 8 pieces (4 whole meatballs) on each sandwich. Top each sandwich with 2 tablespoons of marinara sauce and 2 more slices of cheese.

Put the sandwiches in a heated panini press or on a stovetop grill. Close the press and cook for about 3 minutes, or until the sandwiches are toasty and warmed through. (Alternatively, melt about 1½ tablespoons of unsalted butter in a 12-inch nonstick skillet over medium-high heat. When the butter melts, put the sandwiches in the pan, top with a weight or a small skillet, lower the heat to medium, and cook for 5 to 6 minutes on each side, until the filling is hot.) Serve with the remaining marinara on the side for dipping.

CAN I MAKE MY OWN BREAD CRUMBS?

When I call for bread crumbs in my recipes, I nearly always expect you to use store-bought bread crumbs because they are so handy, but if you don't have any in the cupboard, you can always make your own. Plus, if the recipe says to use "fresh bread crumbs," you have to make them at home. Here's how: Put a slice of bread in the blender or bowl of the food processor fitted with the metal blade and process to crumbs. Easy! Two regular-size slices of bread make about 1 cup of crumbs. If the recipe calls for dried bread crumbs (that is, store-bought), and you want to make these at home, toast or bake the bread in a low oven for 15 to 20 minutes until dry before grinding it. Or, let the slices sit out overnight so that they turn stale.

I NEARLY ALWAYS EXPECT YOU TO USE STORE-BOUGHT BREAD CRUMBS, BUT IF YOU DON'T HAVE ANY, YOU CAN ALWAYS MAKE YOUR OWN.

CATFISH NUGGET SANDWICHES WITH ROASTED PEPPER AND JALAPEÑO RELISH

I happen to like catfish a lot, although I know not everyone does. If you are unsure, try these fried nuggets in this moist sandwich with its overlay of heat. You might very well become a convert. And if you're someone who already likes catfish, this sandwich will fulfill your dreams! The relish balances the crunch of the fish and makes this extra-special. Don't cook the catfish ahead of time if possible, but if you must, wrap it in parchment and keep it warm in the a low oven. This sandwich would be awesome with Tempting Tempura-Fried Okra (page 39).

Serves 4 or 5

ROASTED PEPPER AND JALAPEÑO RELISH:

1 cup finely diced roasted red peppers
2 plum tomatoes, seeded and minced
2 jalapeño chile peppers, minced
2 shallots, minced
1 clove garlic, minced
2 tablespoons extra-virgin olive oil
1 tablespoon sugar
Grated zest of 2 lemons
Juice of 1 lemon

SANDWICHES:

Canola oil, for frying
1 cup all-purpose flour
2 tablespoons smoked paprika
1 tablespoon cayenne pepper
3 large eggs, lightly beaten
3 cups panko bread crumbs
2 pounds catfish fillets, cut into 1-inch chunks
Juice of 1 lemon
Salt and freshly ground black pepper
1 cup Lemon-Pepper-Garlic Mayonnaise (page 180)
4 or 5 torpedo rolls, about 6 inches long each, split
1½ cups arugula leaves

TO MAKE THE ROASTED PEPPER AND JALAPEÑO RELISH: In a medium ceramic, glass, or another nonreactive bowl, mix together the roasted peppers, tomatoes, jalapeños, shallots, garlic, extra-virgin olive oil, sugar, and lemon zest. Add the lemon juice and stir well.

TO MAKE THE SANDWICHES: Pour enough canola oil into a large, heavy pot to reach a depth of 3 inches. Heat the oil over high heat until a deep-fat thermometer reaches a temperature of 350°F.

Put the flour in a shallow bowl and mix with the paprika and cayenne. Put the eggs in another shallow bowl and the panko in a third bowl. Dip the catfish chunks first in the flour, then in the egg, and finally in the panko, making sure they are well coated.

Using long-handled tongs or a slotted spoon, carefully submerge the catfish in the hot oil, a few pieces at a time so you don't crowd the pot, and fry until lightly brown, 2 to 3 minutes. Lift the fish from the oil with the tongs or slotted spoon and transfer to a large plate or baking sheet lined with paper towels to drain. Season to taste with lemon juice, salt, and black pepper while hot. Let the oil return to 350°F between batches.

Assemble the sandwiches by spreading the mayonnaise on both sides of the halved rolls. Spread equal amounts of the relish on the bread, and then put 4 or 5 chunks of catfish in each roll. Top each sandwich with arugula and serve.

IF YOU'RE SOMEONE WHO ALREADY LIKES CATFISH, THIS SANDWICH WILL FULFILL YOUR DREAMS!

BRAISED BBQ PORK BELLY SLIDERS WITH PESTO MAYONNAISE, CHEDDAR CHEESE, AND CARAMELIZED ONIONS

Normally sliders are small burgers, but these, made with pork belly, take the concept to a new level. My buddy Shane worked at Momofuku Noodle Bar, a restaurant on First Avenue in New York, where they serve something similar, and although I was inspired by that sandwich, it is nothing like mine, which is more like an upscale White Castle burger. The little piece of pork fat melts in the mouth.

Serves 8

CARAMELIZED ONIONS:

½ cup (1 stick) unsalted butter
2 medium onions, sliced
2 tablespoons sugar

SANDWICHES:

2 pounds pork belly
Salt and freshly ground black pepper
2 tablespoons canola oil
8 cloves garlic, peeled
1 medium onion, diced
1 cup packed brown sugar
½ cup balsamic vinegar
¼ cup Dijon mustard
2 cups beef broth
2 cups chicken broth
Leaves from one 4- to 5-inch-long sprig fresh rosemary
8 slider rolls, split
2 tablespoons olive oil
8 ounces cheddar cheese, sliced
½ cup Pesto Mayonnaise (page 186)

recipe continued on page 108

TO MAKE THE CARAMELIZED ONIONS: In a large skillet, melt the butter over medium-high heat. When hot, add the onions and cook, stirring, until soft and translucent, 6 to 7 minutes. Sprinkle with the sugar and cook until lightly browned and caramelized, 2 to 4 minutes. Set aside.

Preheat the oven to 375°F.

TO MAKE THE SANDWICHES: With a small, sharp knife, score the fatty side of the pork belly and then cut the pork into 4 equal square pieces. Season lightly with salt and pepper.

In a large Dutch oven or similar pot, heat the canola oil over medium heat. When hot, cook the pork belly, 1 piece at a time and scored side down, until most of the fat renders, about 4 minutes; do not increase the heat or the pork belly will cook too quickly. Remove each piece of pork belly from the pot when cooked.

Drain all but 4 tablespoons of fat from the pot and cook the garlic over medium heat, stirring, until lightly browned, about 1 minute. Add the onion and cook, stirring, until lightly colored, 2 to 3 minutes. Add the brown sugar and vinegar and cook, stirring, until syrupy, 1 to 2 minutes. Whisk in the mustard until smooth. Stir in the beef and chicken broths and the rosemary leaves and bring to a boil over high heat. Add the pork belly, cover the pot, and put in the oven. Braise for 1½ to 2 hours, until the pork is fork-tender. Lift the pork belly from the pot and transfer to a plate. Do not turn off the oven. Discard the cooking liquid.

Brush each halved roll with the olive oil and grill on a heated countertop grill or under a hot broiler for 2 to 3 minutes or until toasty and slightly charred. Cut each square of belly in half and put 1 piece on the bottom half of each slider roll. Top with a few slices of cheese. Put these assembled sandwich halves on a baking sheet and bake for 1 to 2 minutes at 375°F or until the cheese melts and begins to brown. Remove from the oven and top with the caramelized onions. Spread the top halves of the rolls with the mayonnaise and press on top of the onions to close the sandwiches. Serve hot.

NORMALLY SLIDERS ARE SMALL BURGERS, BUT THESE, MADE WITH PORK BELLY, TAKE THE CONCEPT TO A NEW LEVEL.

CUBAN SANDWICHES

This is my version of a Cuban sandwich, and I think it's terrific. The ciabatta rolls hold in the flavors of the pork, pickles, and mustard, so that every bite is as satisfying as the one before. I love this sandwich.

Serves 4

- 4 ciabatta rolls
- ½ cup Mojo Marinade (page 196)
- ½ cup Horseradish Mustard (page 188)
- 8 thick slices Swiss cheese
- 1 large dill pickle, sliced lengthwise into quarters
- 8 thick slices deli ham
- 2 cups Pulled Pork (page 94)
- ¼ cup sliced pickled jalapeño chile peppers, optional
- 2 tablespoons unsalted butter, softened

TO PREPARE: Separate the rolls so that you have 8 halves. Drizzle the marinade on the outside, crusty side of each roll and then spread that side with the mustard. Lay the 4 bottom halves of the rolls, mustard side up, on a work surface.

Put 2 slices of cheese on each bottom roll.

Arrange the pickle slices and ham slices on the bottom half of the bread and then top with the pulled pork. Put the jalapeños on the pork, if desired. Top the sandwiches with the top halves of the rolls, mustard-side down, and press gently.

Spread butter over both sides of each sandwich: Because the sandwich is "inside-out," you will be spreading the butter on the traditional inside of the rolls. Put the sandwiches in a heated panini press. Close the press and cook for 5 to 6 minutes, until the sandwiches are toasty and warmed through. (Alternatively, melt about 1½ tablespoons of unsalted butter in a 12-inch nonstick skillet over medium-high heat. When the butter melts, put the sandwiches in the pan, top with a weight or a small skillet, lower the heat to medium, and cook for 5 to 6 minutes on each side, until the filling is hot.) Serve hot.

GRILLED MARINATED PORTOBELLO MUSHROOM SANDWICHES

I used to own a restaurant called McCargo's in Camden. We were located downtown and had a lot of foot traffic from surrounding offices, the courthouse, and local universities. This meant a nice number of "regulars," including Cheryl and Orion, a couple who became good friends of mine. Cheryl liked the chicken salad sandwich, and Orion preferred red meat. He had never had a mushroom sandwich, but when I suggested this one, he tried it. He loved it and ordered it about three times a week from then on. It's loaded with flavor, and the mushrooms satisfy much like meat.

Serves 4

MARINADE:

8 ounces (1 cup) porter or stout beer
¼ cup olive oil
¼ cup soy sauce
2 tablespoons toasted sesame oil
1 tablespoon minced garlic
1 tablespoon dried oregano
1 tablespoon brown sugar
1 tablespoon crushed red pepper flakes

SANDWICHES:

8 portobello mushrooms, stems removed
4 kaiser rolls, split
2 tablespoons olive oil
1 teaspoon smoked paprika
8 ounces cheddar cheese curds, or 2 cups shredded cheddar cheese
⅔ cup Chipotle Mayonnaise (page 185)
4 thick tomato slices
Bibb lettuce leaves

TO MAKE THE MARINADE: In a large bowl, mix together the beer, olive oil, soy sauce, sesame oil, garlic, oregano, brown sugar, and red pepper flakes.

TO MAKE THE SANDWICHES: Lay the mushrooms in a shallow glass, ceramic, or another nonreactive dish. Pour the marinade over them and turn to make sure they are well coated. Set aside at room temperature for at least 1 hour and up to 4 hours.

Prepare a hot fire in a charcoal or gas grill and oil the grill grates.

Brush the cut sides of the rolls with the olive oil and sprinkle with the paprika. Grill, oiled sides down, until slightly charred, 1 to 2 minutes. Remove and set aside.

Lift the mushrooms from the marinade and grill for about 3 minutes on each side. Baste the mushrooms with the remaining marinade during grilling.

Top 4 of the mushrooms with the cheddar cheese and then set the remaining mushrooms on top of the cheese. Cover the grill and let the mushrooms cook for about 1 minute to partially melt the cheese.

Meanwhile, spread the mayonnaise on each roll and put a mushroom "sandwich" on the bottom half of each roll. Top with a tomato slice, lettuce leaves, and the top of the roll. Serve hot.

THIS SANDWICH IS LOADED WITH FLAVOR, AND THE MUSHROOMS SATISFY MUCH LIKE MEAT.

MY MAIN COURSES

I'M NO DIFFERENT FROM ANYONE ELSE. When I plan a meal, I begin with the main course. This may not always be the best way to do it, but neither you nor I will change human nature, and ordinarily the system works well because it's the main course that is the star attraction of most meals. (Admittedly, when I see some just-picked August tomatoes or glistening late-summer greens in the markets, my taste buds twitch, and I start thinking of a meal to build around them; you probably do the same. But that discussion is for the next chapter!)

This chapter is all about the main event. It may be the first chapter you thumb through when you get your hands on the book. You will run your eye over the recipe titles, seeing what appeals to you and what doesn't. All of these dishes tempt me, of course, and I think once you try a few, you will "get" what I do when I cook. I take a dish that sounds familiar and then jack it up so that its flavors explode and almost spill over the top—but never quite! There is nothing wacky going on, just good plain cooking.

Most of the recipes here are perfect for family meals, while a few may be more suitable for a party. For example, Horseradish-Crusted Filet Mignon with Braised Portobello Mushrooms (page 120) and Stuffed Grilled Boneless Pork Chops with Hickory Bacon, Smoked Gouda, and Marmalade Glaze (page 137) might be a little over the top for a weekday family supper, while the Pepperoni-Cheeseburger Turnovers (page 131) and Jerk Me Sweet Pork Chops (page 134) are just about perfect.

My main courses may be an eclectic mixture of high-end dishes such as the Lollipop Lamb (page 145) and scrappier ones such as Cheddar Biscuits Stuffed with Savory Baked Eggs (page 150) or Barbecue Chicken Penne Melt (page 127). In the notes introducing the recipes, I make suggestions for side dishes that will round out the meal. Follow my guidance or use your own sense of what your family likes.

RECIPES

PERFECT GRILLED SKIRT STEAK

Skirt steak, my favorite for quick grilling, benefits from rubs and marinades. My Meat Seasoning is excellent here. Once the steak is cooked, serve it with the Cheesy Potatoes with Bacon and Oregano (page 167), the Rosemary-Mashed Yukon Gold Potatoes (page 168), or the Toasted Jasmine Rice with Crunchy Bean Sprouts (page 161). The skirt is cut from under the breast of the steer and rarely is thicker than ¾ inch. When you buy skirt steak, ask for the outside cut, which is a little more tender than the inside cut (although they both are terrific).

Serves 4 to 6

¼ cup canola oil
¼ cup Meat Seasoning (page 195)
2 tablespoons chopped garlic
2 tablespoons fresh lemon juice
2 pounds skirt steak, trimmed

TO PREPARE: In a small bowl, mix together the oil, seasoning, garlic, and lemon juice. Rub the mixture on both sides of the meat, making sure to work it into the meat. Let the meat marinate at room temperature for at least 30 minutes but no longer than 45 minutes (if the day is very hot, don't leave the meat out for longer than 30 minutes).

Prepare a hot fire in a charcoal or gas grill and oil the grill grates.

Grill the steak for 3 to 5 minutes on each side, until done to the degree of doneness you prefer. Let the skirt steaks rest for 5 minutes before slicing to serve.

JERK CHICKEN PASTA WITH A SWEET KICK AND BUFFALO CHICKEN PASTA WITH BLUE CHEESE SAUCE

I call the next two recipes one-pot wonders, but they really are so much more: they are crowd-pleasers. I showcased the Buffalo Chicken Pasta with Blue Cheese Sauce (page 118) as part of a demonstration for Barilla Pasta at a festival in California's Napa Valley last year. People lined up to sample it, many of them coming back for seconds and thirds. When I make this at home, my six-year-old son eats the left-overs cold, right from the refrigerator. It's that good. The Jerk Chicken Pasta is similar but has a little more of a kick. You can't go wrong with either of these for potlucks, family celebrations, or any other time you want easy, filling pasta dishes.

JERK CHICKEN PASTA WITH A SWEET KICK

Serves 4

1 pound farfalle (also called bowtie pasta)

½ cup Jerk Seasoning (page 194)

¼ cup canola oil

4 boneless, skinless chicken breasts, each about 8 ounces, pounded lightly

½ cup chicken broth

1 cup thinly sliced carrots

1 cup sliced red cabbage

½ cup (1 stick) unsalted butter, cut into pieces

2 teaspoons chopped scallions, white and green parts

2 tablespoons chopped fresh flat-leaf parsley

TO PREPARE: In a large saucepan, cook the pasta according to the package directions until al dente. Drain and set aside.

In a large, shallow bowl, stir together 2 tablespoons of the jerk seasoning and 2 tablespoons of the oil. Put the chicken breasts in the mixture and turn several times to coat evenly on both sides. Set aside at room temperature for 20 to 30 minutes, or cover and refrigerate for 8 hours or overnight.

In a large skillet, heat the remaining 2 tablespoons of oil over medium-high heat. Sear the chicken breasts until cooked through, 2 to 3 minutes per side. Set aside to cool, and when cool enough to handle, dice the meat into small pieces.

Add the pasta and ½ cup of the broth to the skillet and heat until hot. Add the remaining 6 tablespoons of jerk seasoning to the pasta and toss to mix. Add the chicken, carrots, and cabbage and stir until heated. Remove the skillet from the heat and stir in the butter until melted. Stir in the scallions and parsley and serve immediately.

NOTE: You will notice that I often pound chicken breasts until they are thin before I cook them. This allows them to cook quickly, so that they stay flavorful and juicy.

To pound chicken breasts, put them between two pieces of plastic wrap and lay them on a work surface. Using a meat mallet, gently pound the chicken, moving the mallet around on the meat to achieve an equal thickness. Don't actually pound the chicken, but work with small, gentle hits that are harder than a tap but softer than a wallop!

I also use the small grooved side of the mallet, but you have to be very careful that it does not tear the plastic. Of course, you don't have to use the plastic wrap, but it does keep the chicken contained and the whole process neater.

Chicken breasts and other cuts of meat also can be pounded with the flat side of a small cast-iron pan or a similar improvised tool.

BUFFALO CHICKEN PASTA WITH BLUE CHEESE SAUCE

Serves 6

1 pound campanelle or other sturdy, shaped pasta

1½ cups heavy cream

½ cup hot pepper sauce (I use Durkee hot sauce)

2 tablespoons chopped garlic

1 teaspoon coarsely ground black pepper

½ teaspoon cayenne pepper, optional

Salt

4 cups coarsely chopped store-bought rotisserie chicken (one 3-pound chicken or two 1½-pound chickens)

1¼ cups crumbled blue cheese

¼ cup chopped scallions, white and green parts

TO PREPARE: In a large saucepan, cook the pasta according to the package directions until al dente. Drain, do not rinse, and set aside.

In another large saucepan, heat the heavy cream, hot pepper sauce, garlic, black pepper, and cayenne, if using, over medium heat, stirring until blended. Season to taste with salt. Add the hot pasta and chicken and stir until well coated and warmed through.

Remove the pasta from the heat and stir in the blue cheese and scallions. Serve immediately.

HORSERADISH-CRUSTED FILET MIGNON WITH BRAISED PORTOBELLO MUSHROOMS

When my brother Donavon and I were cooking together about a year ago, I asked him to grate some fresh horseradish for a sauce. Now, Donavon and I often grill together and enjoy our time hanging out by the fire and cooking thick steaks, burgers, chicken, or whatever, but I had never, until that day, seen my brother cry. Of course it was the sharp, pungent horseradish that was the cause of his tears, but I couldn't stand it! I immediately changed the recipe to include bread crumbs, mushrooms, and prepared horseradish. I mean, who wants to see his brother weep?

Serves 4

STEAKS:

½ cup prepared horseradish
¼ cup spicy brown mustard
3 tablespoons minced garlic
2 tablespoons olive oil
2 tablespoons cracked black pepper, plus more as needed
Four 6-ounce filets mignons
Coarse sea salt or smoked salt
¾ cup panko bread crumbs
1 tablespoon canola oil

PORTOBELLOS:

2 tablespoons unsalted butter
4 portobello mushroom caps, cut into ¼-inch-thick slices
1 teaspoon salt
1 teaspoon cracked black pepper
1 tablespoon minced garlic
½ cup red wine
¼ cup beef broth
1 tablespoon sherry vinegar
1 tablespoon chopped fresh thyme

recipe continued on page 122

TO COOK THE STEAKS: Preheat the oven to 400°F.

In a medium bowl, whisk together the horseradish, mustard, garlic, olive oil, and pepper. Season the steaks with salt and more pepper and coat both sides with the mustard mixture. Dip the steaks in panko to coat on both sides.

In a large skillet, heat the canola oil over medium-high heat and sear the steaks for 2 minutes on each side. Lift the steaks from the skillet and set aside on a rack set in a baking pan.

TO COOK THE PORTOBELLOS: Drain any excess oil from the skillet and then melt the butter in the skillet over medium-high heat. Add the mushrooms to the skillet and season with the salt and pepper. Cook, stirring, until the mushrooms soften and color slightly, 3 to 4 minutes. Add the garlic to the pan and stir into the butter and exuded juices from the mushrooms. Add the wine and broth, stir, and cook for about 3 minutes to reduce slightly. Spoon the sauce over the mushrooms to coat them. Stir in the vinegar and thyme.

Meanwhile, cook the steaks in the oven for about 5 minutes for medium-rare, or until cooked to the desired doneness and until the breading browns. Let the steaks rest for about 5 minutes before serving with the mushrooms spooned over them.

BLACK AND TAN TILAPIA WITH ANCHOVY-LEMON BUTTER

Tilapia is a mild freshwater fish that is easily farm raised and therefore relatively inexpensive compared to other fish. It has become commonplace in our markets but, because it is no longer "the new thing," I fear it's lost a little of its love, too. If you haven't tried it in a while, don't let another day go by. Because it's so mild, it needs some saltiness, which is why the anchovies and lemon work so well with it; you don't need anything more. Even if you think of yourself as anchovy-phobic, don't shy away from this recipe. The little fish and the lemon melt over the tilapia and mellow out. You will love this dish. It would taste wonderful with the Rosemary-Mashed Yukon Gold Potatoes (page 168) or the Savory Sage, Prosciutto, and Fontina Orzo (page 169).

Serves 4

- 5 tablespoons olive oil
- ¼ cup chopped anchovy fillets
- ¼ cup fresh lemon juice (1 to 2 lemons)
- 4 tablespoons unsalted butter
- 1 tablespoon chopped fresh cilantro
- Pinch of freshly ground black pepper
- Four 6-ounce tilapia fillets
- 2 tablespoons Chesapeake Spice Blend (page 190)
- 2 tablespoons finely grated lemon zest

TO PREPARE: In a small skillet, heat 1 tablespoon of the olive oil over medium heat, and when hot, add the anchovies and cook, stirring, until they break apart, about 1 minute. Add the lemon juice and cook, stirring, until the lemon juice reduces slightly, 3 to 4 minutes. Add the butter, cilantro, and pepper, remove from the heat, and stir until the butter melts. Set aside, covered, to keep warm.

Preheat a countertop grill or set a cast-iron grill pan over medium-high heat.

Rub the fish on all sides with the remaining 4 tablespoons olive oil and then sprinkle evenly with the spice blend and lemon zest. Grill on the hot grill or grill pan until cooked through, 2½ to 3 minutes per side. Serve immediately, with the anchovy butter spooned over each fillet.

SUN-DRIED TOMATO, BASIL, BACON, AND GRUYÈRE CHEESE OMELET

I have always been a fan of breakfast for dinner. As kids, it was not uncommon for Mom to give us pancakes or biscuits and gravy for supper, and I happily have carried the tradition into my adult life. It's not unusual for me to make omelets with whatever is in the refrigerator for a tasty evening meal; no one complains. I developed this one shortly after I had made the Cordon Bleu–Style Fritters with Dijon Mustard–Gruyère Cheese Sauce on page 38 and had some Gruyère cheese left over. I think the cheese makes a big difference here, just as it does with the fritters. My family particularly likes this dish in the summertime because it's nice and light.

Serves 3

6 large eggs
1 tablespoon kosher salt
1 tablespoon freshly ground black pepper
1 teaspoon crushed red pepper flakes
1 cup shredded Gruyère cheese
½ cup drained and chopped oil-packed sun-dried tomatoes
8 slices bacon, cooked until crispy and crumbled
¼ cup whole or julienned fresh basil leaves
2 tablespoons canola oil

TO PREPARE: Preheat the oven to 400°F.

In a medium bowl, vigorously beat the eggs with the salt, black pepper, and red pepper flakes for 4 to 5 minutes, until frothy.

In another medium bowl, stir together the cheese, sun-dried tomatoes, bacon, and basil.

In a 12-inch ovenproof skillet, heat the olive oil over medium heat. Add the beaten eggs and cook gently, tilting the pan so that the uncooked egg slides under the more cooked parts. After 2 to 3 minutes, the eggs will begin to set. Sprinkle the cheese mixture evenly over the eggs and remove the pan from the heat.

Transfer the pan to the oven and cook for 3 to 4 minutes, until the cheese melts. Slide the omelet onto a serving platter, folding it over on itself as you do. Let the omelet sit for about 1½ minutes, and then cut and serve.

WHAT IS ROTISSERIE CHICKEN?

I am wild about rotisserie chicken because there are so many dishes you can make with cooked chicken—and how much easier does it get than having someone else cook the chicken for you? At nearly every supermarket I have visited, the deli or prepared food department offers freshly cooked rotisserie chicken. And they are good! The birds may be flavored with all sorts of spices and seasoning, but in reality it doesn't really matter which you buy because for my recipes you are going to remove the skin, which holds these flavors, and chop up the meat. Buy the plumpest chicken you see and take it home for some good cookin'!

BARBECUE CHICKEN PENNE MELT

When you are in the mood for a pasta casserole, try this one, which is easy to make and bursts with great flavors. Because I am nearly always in the mood, I created this recipe so that we could have it just about any old time. When we were growing up and my mom served baked ziti, we kids went bananas, and this is nothing more than a variation of that popular family meal. Don't skimp on the sauce, because the pasta keeps absorbing it as it bakes and if you don't have enough, the final dish will be dry.

Serves 6

- 1 pound mini penne
- 2 tablespoons plus 2 teaspoons unsalted butter
- 1 tablespoon olive oil
- 2 cups diced onions
- 4 to 6 cups shredded store-bought rotisserie chicken (one 3-pound chicken or two 1½-pound chickens)
- 1 quart bottled hickory-smoked flavored barbecue sauce
- 12 slices bacon, cooked until crispy and crumbled
- ½ cup chopped scallions, white and green parts
- 1½ cups shredded mozzarella cheese
- 2 cups shredded sharp cheddar cheese

TO PREPARE: In a medium saucepan, cook the pasta according to the package directions until al dente. Drain, do not rinse, and set aside.

In a medium skillet, heat the butter and oil over medium-high heat and, when hot, add the onions and cook, stirring, until softened and starting to brown, about 5 minutes.

Preheat the oven to 375°F. Grease an 11 by 9-inch baking dish.

In a large bowl, toss the pasta with the chicken, 3½ cups of the barbecue sauce, the bacon, scallions, and cooked onions. In another bowl, stir together the cheeses.

Spread one-third of the pasta mixture in the prepared dish and top with one-third of the cheese. Make two more layers of pasta and cheese, cover with aluminum foil, and bake for 30 minutes. Remove the foil and continue to bake for another 10 to 15 minutes, until the cheese is browned. Remove from the oven, drizzle with the remaining ½ cup barbecue sauce, and serve.

CORNED BEEF REUBEN CASSEROLE

Years ago I was hired to cater a St. Patrick's Day party, and when I asked if I could try something a little different from traditional corned beef and cabbage, I got an enthusiastic nod. This casserole is a good way to serve a lot of people and still keep the spirit and luck o' the Irish alive and well. Of course, I like this just about anytime; it does not have to wait for March 17.

Serves 6 to 8

- 1 cup drained sauerkraut
- 1 cup Thousand Island Dressing (page 177)
- 3 cups Aaron's Mashed Potatoes (page 165)
- 1¾ pounds lean cooked corned beef, diced (about 4 cups)
- 2 cups shredded Swiss cheese

TO PREPARE: Preheat the oven to 375°F.

In a medium bowl, combine the sauerkraut and Thousand Island dressing.

In a 1½-quart casserole, spread half the mashed potatoes. Top with half the corned beef, half the cheese, and half the sauerkraut mixture. Repeat to make another layer, ending with the sauerkraut mixture.

Bake, uncovered, for 20 to 25 minutes, until crispy on top.

PEPPERONI-CHEESEBURGER TURNOVERS

I was asked to develop some recipes for some mighty tasty thick-cut bacon from Tyson Foods called Wright Brand bacon. I used the bacon in the Stuffed Grilled Boneless Pork Chops with Hickory Bacon, Smoked Gouda, and Marmalade Glaze (page 137) and loved it, but when I added it to one of my super-juicy, full-flavored cheeseburgers, I knew I had a home run.

Serves 4

- 3 tablespoons canola oil
- 8 ounces ground beef
- 2 tablespoons chopped fresh oregano
- 2 tablespoons granulated garlic powder
- 2 tablespoons granulated onion powder
- 1 teaspoon coarse salt
- 1 teaspoon coarsely ground black pepper
- ½ cup coarsely chopped cooked thick-cut bacon (about 12 slices)
- 1 pound store-bought pizza dough
- 1½ cups shredded fontina cheese
- 1½ cups shredded mozzarella cheese
- 1 cup diced onion
- 1 cup Easy Marinara Sauce (page 200) or store-bought pizza sauce
- ½ cup chopped scallions, white and green parts
- ½ cup chopped pepperoni

TO PREPARE: Preheat the oven to 375°F.

In a large skillet, heat 1 tablespoon of the oil over medium heat. When hot, add the ground beef, breaking it up with a wooden spoon. Add the oregano, garlic powder, onion powder, salt, and pepper and stir well to mix. Cook the mixture, stirring, until the beef is well browned, 4 to 5 minutes. Drain the fat from the pan, stir in the bacon, and set the mixture aside to cool.

Cut the pizza dough into quarters and, on a lightly floured surface, roll each quarter into a 5- to 6-inch diameter circle.

Stir the cheeses, onion, marinara, scallions, and pepperoni into the cooled beef mixture. Spoon about ½ cup of the mixture on one half of each circle of dough. Fold the dough over the filling into a half-moon and pinch the edges to seal.

Arrange the turnovers on a baking sheet, cut a few slits in them, and bake for 20 to 25 minutes, until lightly browned and thoroughly heated. Serve hot or warm.

NOTE: Alternatively, the turnovers may be deep-fried in 375°F oil for 5 to 6 minutes; turn to brown evenly and drain on paper towels.

BROCCOLI RABE AND ARTICHOKE PASTA

This is a spectacular vegetarian dish for a potluck or any time you want to serve a lot of people (you can double the recipe easily), but the first time I made it was not for a big party. I made it for my wife, Kimberly, who was intimidated by broccoli rabe, thinking it too bitter for her taste. I added it to warm pasta with the other ingredients and presto! Kim was won over. Since then she has been a big fan of this pasta in particular and broccoli rabe in general. I always make extra because she takes it to work to eat for lunch. She likes it as much cold as she does hot!

Serves 4 to 6

1 pound farfalle (also called bowtie pasta)
2 pounds broccoli rabe
⅔ cup olive oil
2 tablespoons unsalted butter
1 cup thinly sliced red onion
2 tablespoons chopped garlic
1 teaspoon crushed red pepper flakes
One 1-ounce envelope onion soup mix
Two 12-ounce cans marinated artichoke hearts, quartered, marinade reserved
¼ cup fresh lemon juice (1 to 2 lemons)
Grated zest of 1 lemon
Kosher salt and freshly ground black pepper
½ cup grated Romano cheese

TO PREPARE: In a medium saucepan, cook the pasta according to the package directions until al dente. Drain, reserving ¼ cup of the pasta water.

Fill a large saucepan about halfway full with water and bring to a boil over high heat. Meanwhile, fill a large bowl with cold water and ice. Immerse the broccoli rabe in the boiling water and blanch for 30 seconds. Drain and immediately plunge the broccoli rabe in the ice water to stop the cooking. When cool, drain thoroughly on paper towels, and chop.

In a large skillet, heat ⅓ cup of the olive oil and the butter over high heat. When the butter melts, add the onion and cook, stirring, until it begins to soften, 2 to 3 minutes. Add the garlic, red pepper flakes, onion soup mix, and chopped broccoli rabe. Continue to cook, stirring, until heated through.

Add the reserved pasta water and stir in the artichokes and their marinade, the lemon juice, and lemon zest. Add the pasta and toss to mix. Season to taste with salt and pepper. Heat through and transfer to a serving platter. Top with the remaining ⅓ cup of olive oil and the cheese, and serve.

BLACKENED COD WITH BLUE CHEESE SAUCE

Way back in the 1990s, I was working in a fine-dining restaurant, and my boss gave me a chance to create a dish. Because I had always liked Buffalo chicken wings and blue cheese, I suggested pairing those flavors with cod. At first the chef was hesitant, but even though he didn't think it would fly, he told me to go for it. For that dish, I added some crabmeat to the sauce, but for the home kitchen I have simplified it. There is something about the sharpness of the cheese against the spiciness and crunch of the blackened fish that works beautifully. For the best outcome, be sure to have a thick, center-cut piece of cod.

Serves 6

BLUE CHEESE SAUCE:

- ½ cup dry white wine
- ¾ cup heavy cream
- 1¼ cups crumbled blue cheese

COD:

- 3 tablespoons paprika
- 3 tablespoons salt
- 2 tablespoons cayenne pepper
- 1½ tablespoons Italian Herb Blend (page 193)
- 1½ teaspoons freshly cracked black pepper
- Six 6-ounce boneless, skinless pieces of cod
- 3 tablespoons unsalted butter
- 1½ tablespoons canola oil

TO PREPARE: Preheat the oven to 400°F.

TO MAKE THE SAUCE: In a medium saucepan, bring the wine to a boil over medium-high heat. Lower the heat and simmer until the wine reduces by half, 2 to 3 minutes. Stir in the heavy cream and bring to a simmer. Let the mixture cook until reduced again by half, 6 to 7 minutes. Stir in the blue cheese and whisk until smooth. Cover to keep warm while you cook the cod.

TO MAKE THE COD: In a small bowl, mix together the paprika, salt, cayenne, Italian herb blend, and black pepper. Lay the cod on a work surface and rub the spice mixture into all sides of the fish. Do not press too hard, but work it in so that it adheres to the flesh.

Heat a large ovenproof skillet over medium-high heat and, when hot, melt the butter with the oil. Cook the cod for about 2 minutes on each side.

Transfer the skillet to the oven and cook for another 4 to 6 minutes, until the cod is cooked through and nearly flaking. Serve the cod with the sauce spooned over the top.

JERK ME SWEET PORK CHOPS

Everyone has heard of and most likely tasted jerk chicken, which has its culinary roots in sunny Jamaica, but who has heard of jerk pork chops? I love the way these chops taste when seasoned with my jerk seasoning, and with the first bite you will be transported to whatever island you choose.

Serves 4

¼ cup plus 2 tablespoons canola oil
Four 8- to 10-ounce thick pork chops
¼ cup Jerk Seasoning (page 194)
¼ cup diced red onion
1 jalapeño chile pepper, diced
2 cups cubed fresh pineapple
½ cup peach preserves
1 teaspoon lemon-pepper seasoning

TO PREPARE: Preheat the oven to 375°F. Prepare a medium-hot to hot fire in a charcoal or gas grill and oil the grill grates.

Rub the ¼ cup of oil over both sides of the pork chops and then sprinkle them with the jerk seasoning, rubbing it into the meat. Grill the chops for 4 to 5 minutes on each side.

Transfer the chops to a baking pan and bake for 8 to 10 minutes.

Meanwhile, in a medium skillet, heat the remaining 2 tablespoons of oil over medium-high heat. Add the onion, jalapeño, and pineapple cubes and cook, stirring, until the onion begins to soften, about 5 minutes. Add the peach preserves and lemon-pepper seasoning, decrease the heat to low, and cook, stirring occasionally, until the sauce comes together, 5 to 10 minutes longer. Serve the sauce with the pork chops.

STUFFED GRILLED BONELESS PORK CHOPS WITH HICKORY BACON, SMOKED GOUDA, AND MARMALADE GLAZE

Years ago I worked at an upscale restaurant in Cherry Hill, New Jersey, called Steak 38, that sold a good number of stuffed veal chops every night. I had never tried them before having that job, but now not only am I an admirer of stuffed veal chops, I am also crazy about stuffed pork chops!

Serves 6

- 1 cup orange marmalade
- ¼ cup chopped scallions, white and green parts
- ¼ cup soy sauce
- ¼ cup spicy chile oil
- 9 ounces fresh baby spinach
- 6 slices hickory bacon, cooked and coarsely chopped (about ½ cup)
- 6 ounces smoked Gouda cheese, cut into small cubes
- 1 tablespoon chopped chipotle chile peppers in adobo sauce
- Six 8-ounce boneless pork loin chops
- Kosher salt and freshly ground black pepper
- 2 tablespoons canola oil

TO PREPARE: In a small bowl, stir together the marmalade, scallions, soy sauce, and chile oil. Set half the marmalade sauce aside for cooking and the other half for serving.

Prepare a hot fire in a charcoal or gas grill and oil the grill grates.

In a large saucepan with a tight-fitting lid, bring about 1 inch of water to a simmer over medium-high heat. Steam the spinach in a steaming basket set in the saucepan until wilted, about 2½ minutes. (Alternatively, wilt the spinach in a microwave-safe bowl covered with plastic wrap. Microwave on high power for 2 to 3 minutes.) Lift the spinach from the steaming basket and transfer to a large bowl. Add the bacon, cheese, and chipotle chiles, and mix well.

With a small, sharp knife, slit the side of each chop to create a pocket that goes nearly but not all the way through the chop. Wiggle the knife in the incision to open the pocket.

Using a spoon or your fingers, stuff each chop with the spinach filling. Secure the openings with toothpicks and then season the chops with salt and pepper. Brush both sides of the chops with the canola oil.

Grill the chops for 6 to 8 minutes with the grill covered, turning the chops 3 times during grilling. Remove the lid and brush the tops of the chops with the marmalade sauce for cooking. Continue grilling, turning once and brushing the other side with the marmalade sauce for cooking, until both sides of each chop are nicely browned and cooked through, 2 to 4 minutes longer. Remove the chops from the grill and let them rest for 10 minutes before serving with the reserved sauce.

HOT-AND-SPICY TURKEY CHOPS PIZZAIOLA

My friend Phil and I were walking through the Reading Terminal Market in the center of Philadelphia, which is a favorite pastime of mine. The market is one of the largest and oldest farmer's markets in the country and is open all year long. I always find something there I have not known about previously, and this day was no exception. We spied "turkey chops" at a meat counter, which fascinated both of us. We had to try them. Because I was in the mood for pizza, when we got home, I created this dish. It's a winner! If you cannot find already-cut turkey chops, ask your butcher to cut chops from a turkey breast for you. If that's not possible, you can make this dish with chicken breasts.

Serves 6

CHOP SEASONING:

- 2 tablespoons kosher salt
- 2 tablespoons smoked paprika
- 2 tablespoons granulated garlic powder
- 1 tablespoon granulated onion powder
- 1 tablespoon freshly ground black pepper
- 1 teaspoon dried oregano
- 1½ cups all-purpose flour

CHOPS:

- Six 8-ounce turkey chops, or 3 whole chicken breasts cut to make chops (see Note)
- ¼ cup canola oil
- 2 tablespoons olive oil
- 2 cups sliced red bell peppers
- 2 cups sliced Italian long green hot peppers
- 1 cup sliced white onion
- 3 cups canned diced tomatoes and their juice
- ¼ cup chopped garlic
- 2 tablespoons kosher salt
- 1 teaspoon crushed red pepper flakes
- 1 tablespoon fresh oregano leaves
- 1 tablespoon fresh basil leaves
- 1 tablespoon freshly ground black pepper
- 16 thick slices smoked fresh mozzarella cheese
- ½ cup chopped scallions, white and green parts

TO PREPARE: Preheat the oven to 350°F.

TO MAKE THE SEASONING: In a shallow dish, mix together the salt, paprika, garlic powder, onion powder, black pepper, and oregano. Remove from the dish one-quarter of the seasoning mix and set aside. Add the flour to the dish and toss with the remaining three-quarters of the mix.

TO COOK THE CHOPS: Toss the chops in the flour-seasoning mixture, so that they are lightly coated. Sprinkle with the reserved seasoning mix.

In a large, deep skillet, heat the canola oil over medium-high heat and cook the chops until golden brown, 2 to 3 minutes per side. As each one is browned, transfer it to a baking dish large enough to hold them in a single layer.

Drain the excess canola oil from the skillet and add the olive oil. When hot, cook the bell peppers, hot peppers, and onion, stirring, until the onions are translucent but not soft, 4 to 5 minutes. Add the tomatoes and their juice, garlic, salt, red pepper flakes, oregano, basil, and black pepper and cook until the mixture begins to bubble and boil and is heated through, about 10 minutes.

Pour the sauce over the chops and top with the mozzarella cheese. Bake for 15 to 20 minutes, until the cheese melts and is golden brown. Top with the scallions and serve.

NOTE: Turkey chops are cut from the whole turkey breast and contain part of the breastbone and the skin. To make "chicken chops" that resemble turkey chops, cut a whole chicken breast (wings removed) straight down through the breastbone to make 2 chops. Each chop will be connected to the breastbone. (This way of cutting the whole breast is the exact opposite of how chicken breasts usually are cut into halves, when the halves are separated by cutting along the breastbone.)

CHICKEN CORDON BLEU BUNDLES AND SALISBURY STEAK BUNDLES

The last job I had before I won *The Next Food Network Star* competition was in the catering department at Thomas Jefferson Hospital in Philadelphia. I was asked to come up with a holiday dish that looked fancy and festive but was easy for patients to chew and swallow. I first made these bundles with black beans but have since added chicken to one version and Salisbury steak to another—with lip-smacking results! Be sure to serve these with a side or two, such as a green salad or lightly cooked vegetables, because otherwise the bundles look naked on the plate. These also make tasty appetizers.

BE SURE TO SERVE THESE WITH A SIDE OR TWO BECAUSE OTHERWISE THEY LOOK NAKED ON THE PLATE.

CHICKEN CORDON BLEU BUNDLES

Serves 4

4 whole scallions, trimmed
1¼ cups diced low-sodium cooked ham
½ cup torn or coarsely chopped cooked chicken breast
¼ cup diced Swiss cheese
1 tablespoon diced shallots
1 tablespoon sliced scallions, white and green parts
1 tablespoon all-purpose flour
1½ teaspoons salt
1 teaspoon coarsely ground black pepper
4 sheets phyllo dough (see page 146)
½ cup (1 stick) unsalted butter, melted

TO PREPARE: Preheat the oven to 400°F.

In a wide skillet filled with simmering water over medium-high heat, blanch the whole scallions until softened, 2 to 3 minutes. (Alternatively, soften the scallions in a microwave-safe dish covered with plastic wrap. Microwave on high power for 2 to 3 minutes.) Drain and set aside to cool.

In a large bowl, toss together the ham, chicken, cheese, shallots, sliced scallions, flour, salt, and pepper.

Brush each sheet of phyllo dough with melted butter and stack the sheets. Cut the phyllo stack into quarters, and spoon equal amounts of the ham-chicken mixture in the center of each quarter. Pull the corners of the quarters up over the filling and tie them closed with the blanched scallions. Brush the bundles with melted butter. Arrange the bundles on a baking sheet and bake for 8 to 10 minutes, until golden brown and the filling is heated through.

SALISBURY STEAK BUNDLES

Serves 4

SALISBURY STEAK:

1 pound ground beef
1 large egg, lightly beaten
½ cup seeded and diced red bell pepper
½ cup seeded and diced green bell pepper
¼ cup bread crumbs
1 tablespoon Worcestershire sauce
½ teaspoon fresh thyme leaves
½ teaspoon fresh oregano leaves
¼ teaspoon salt
¼ teaspoon freshly ground black pepper

GRAVY:

4 tablespoons unsalted butter
¼ cup all-purpose flour
2 cups beef broth
½ teaspoon torn fresh sage leaves
½ teaspoon fresh thyme leaves
½ teaspoon fresh oregano leaves

BUNDLES:

12 whole scallions, trimmed
12 sheets phyllo dough (see page 146)
¾ cup (1½ sticks) unsalted butter, melted
2 cups Aaron's Mashed Potatoes (page 165)

TO MAKE THE SALISBURY STEAK: Preheat the oven to 350°F.

In a large bowl, mix together the ground beef, egg, bell peppers, bread crumbs, Worcestershire sauce, thyme, oregano, salt, and black pepper. When thoroughly mixed, form the meat into 12 oval-shaped portions and transfer them to a baking sheet. Bake for about 15 minutes, or until cooked through. Let the Salisbury steak ovals cool. Lower the oven temperature to 300°F.

TO MAKE THE GRAVY: In a saucepan, whisk the butter with the flour over medium heat until blended and smooth. Add the broth, sage, thyme, and oregano and bring to a boil over high heat. Lower the heat to medium-high and simmer until the gravy thickens slightly, 6 to 8 minutes. Remove from the heat and set aside, covered, to keep warm.

TO MAKE THE BUNDLES: In a wide skillet filled with simmering water over medium-high heat, blanch the scallions until softened, 1 to 2 minutes. (Alternatively, soften the scallions in a microwave-safe dish covered with plastic wrap. Microwave on high power for 2 to 3 minutes.) Drain and set aside to cool.

Brush each sheet of phyllo dough with melted butter and make 4 stacks of 3 sheets each. Cut each phyllo stack into quarters so that you have 16 stacks.

Put a Salisbury steak oval onto the center of each stack and top with a scoop of potatoes. Pull the corners of the quarters up over the filling and tie them closed with the blanched scallions. Brush the bundles with melted butter. Arrange the bundles on a baking sheet and bake for 6 to 8 minutes, or until golden brown and the filling is heated through. Serve the bundles with the gravy, reheated gently, if necessary.

BACON-WRAPPED ZUCCHINI STUFFED WITH CORNBREAD AND CRAB

One November I found myself with some leftover cornbread from the Thanksgiving turkey stuffing, and when my sister stopped by, we decided to stuff zucchini with it. And why not add some succulent crab, we asked ourselves? When the dish was done, it was spectacular, but we weren't sure whether it would be better as a main course or as an appetizer. I put it in this chapter because it's filling and completed by the crabmeat, but either way, it's a star. I like to say that zucchini comes back to life when cooked this way!

Serves 6

6 store-bought corn muffins, crumbled
4 tablespoons unsalted butter, melted
¼ cup chopped scallions, white and green parts
2 tablespoons chopped fresh flat-leaf parsley
2 tablespoons Chesapeake Spice Blend (page 190)
One 1-pound can jumbo lump crabmeat, picked over for shells
6 medium zucchini, each squash about 6 inches long
12 slices bacon

TO PREPARE: Preheat the oven to 400°F.

In a large bowl, mix the crumbled corn muffins with the butter, scallions, parsley, and spice blend. Stir well and then gently fold the crabmeat into the mixture, taking care not to break up the crab too much.

Split the zucchini in half lengthwise. Scoop out the seeds and a little of the flesh to make a shallow indentation in each half. Spoon an equal amount of the crab mixture into each zucchini half. Wrap a bacon strip around each stuffed half and arrange them, seam side down, on a baking sheet. (You can also secure the bacon with toothpicks.) Bake for 20 to 25 minutes, until the bacon is crispy and the filling is heated through.

LOLLIPOP LAMB

I love how the chef at Brio Tuscan Grille in Cherry Hill, New Jersey, cooks lamb, so I asked my friend Barry, who manages the restaurant, about it. He explained how they cook their lamb chops and I tried to duplicate it—with some McCargo flavor additions. I frenched the bones, which means I scraped all the meat off the long bones so that the small, luscious nugget at the end of each chop could be eaten "like a lollipop." I love this, and while it's a great main course, you could easily serve it as a hot appetizer.

Serves 4

- **1 cup cooked, crumbled mild-flavored pork sausage, such as Italian**
- **¾ cup chopped smoked fresh mozzarella cheese**
- **½ cup diced jarred roasted red peppers**
- **½ cup seasoned Italian bread crumbs**
- **¼ cup chopped scallions, white and green parts**
- **2 tablespoons chopped garlic**
- **Kosher salt and freshly ground black pepper**
- **1 rack of lamb with 12 chops, frenched**
- **½ cup extra-virgin olive oil**

TO PREPARE: Prepare a hot fire in a charcoal or gas grill and oil the grill grates. Preheat the oven to 375°F.

In a large bowl, mix together the sausage, mozzarella, roasted peppers, bread crumbs, scallions, and garlic. Add about 1 teaspoon of salt and 1 teaspoon of black pepper; mix well and set aside.

Slice the chops apart. With a small, sharp knife, slit the side of each lamb chop to create a pocket that goes nearly but not all the way through the chop. Wiggle the knife in the incision to open the pocket.

Using a spoon or your fingers, stuff each chop with the sausage filling. Secure the openings with toothpicks and then season the chops with salt and pepper. Brush both sides of the chops with the extra-virgin olive oil.

Put the chops on the hot grill and cook for about 2 minutes on each side to make nice grill marks. Transfer to a small baking dish and bake for 2 to 5 minutes, until cooked through and an instant-read thermometer inserted in the thickest part of the chops registers 135°F. Remove the chops from the oven, let them rest for about 5 minutes, and serve.

WHERE DO I BUY PHYLLO DOUGH?

Phyllo dough is sold in the frozen food department of just about every supermarket in the country. You can also buy it fresh at some Middle Eastern markets, high-end gourmet shops, and health food stores. Most of us purchase it frozen in 1-pound packages, which hold about 20 large sheets of dough. Typically these measure about 12 inches wide and 18 inches long. When you look for it in the market, remember that it's also called filo dough or fillo dough.

Keep the phyllo in the freezer until you need it, and then let it thaw in the refrigerator. Allow it to come to room temperature before you begin to work with it, and when you do take it out of the package, set it on a clean surface and keep it covered with a damp, well-wrung kitchen towel to prevent it from drying out. The phyllo sheets, which must be stacked and brushed with melted butter or olive oil before they are baked, turn crisp and flaky in the oven.

PHYLLO-WRAPPED CHICKEN AND EGGS WITH RANCHERO SAUCE

This is a straightforward recipe that is great for brunch or lunch, although certainly you could eat it for dinner, too. It's endlessly versatile. You can switch out the chicken for shrimp or steak; the ranchero sauce goes well with all three options. And if you want this to be vegetarian, substitute asparagus or spinach and mushrooms for the chicken.

Serves 5

RANCHERO SAUCE:

3 tablespoons olive oil

½ medium onion, chopped

2 tablespoons minced garlic

1¼ cups canned diced fire-roasted tomatoes

One 4.5-ounce can diced green Anaheim chiles

2 chipotle chile peppers in adobo sauce, minced with 2 teaspoons adobo sauce

2 teaspoons ground cumin

1 teaspoon salt

1 teaspoon freshly ground black pepper

¼ bunch fresh cilantro (6 to 8 sprigs), chopped

CHICKEN AND EGGS:

2 cups coarsely chopped cooked chicken

1 cup shredded cheddar cheese

2 tablespoons canola oil

6 large eggs, beaten

5 sheets phyllo dough (see page 146)

½ cup fresh bread crumbs

4 tablespoons unsalted butter, melted

1 recipe Zesty Guacamole (page 198)

recipe continued on page 148

TO MAKE THE RANCHERO SAUCE: In a medium saucepan, heat the olive oil over medium-high heat. When hot, add the onion and garlic and cook, stirring, until the onion softens, about 2 minutes. Add the tomatoes, green chiles, and chipotle chiles and cook, stirring constantly, for about 2 minutes longer. Add the cumin, salt, and pepper and cook until well incorporated and slightly reduced, 3 to 4 minutes. Stir in the cilantro, cover the pan, and set aside to keep warm.

TO PREPARE THE CHICKEN AND EGGS: In a large bowl, toss the chicken with ¾ cup of the cheese and set aside.

In a large nonstick skillet, heat the canola oil over medium heat. Scramble the eggs until very lightly cooked and still a little runny, 3 to 4 minutes. Remove from the heat and set aside.

Preheat the oven to 450°F.

Unwrap the phyllo dough and put the stack on a plate and cover it with a piece of parchment paper. Place a damp, well-wrung kitchen towel on top of the parchment to help hold it in place. This keeps the phyllo from drying out as you work. Working with 1 sheet at a time, lay the phyllo on a work surface that is spread with bread crumbs and brush the phyllo well with melted butter. Repeat with 4 more sheets of phyllo and create a stack of 5 sheets.

Spread the eggs along the phyllo, leaving a 2-inch border on all sides. Top the stack with an equal amount of the chicken and cheese mixture and roll the phyllo stack into a log. Using your finger, rub a little melted butter along the edge of the phyllo and seal the log closed. Brush the log with more butter and transfer to a baking sheet or shallow baking pan.

Repeat 4 more times to make a total of 5 logs.

Bake the phyllo logs for 10 to 12 minutes, until nicely browned. Remove the logs from the hot pan and let them cool for about 1 minute. Cut the log into 10 pieces. Serve with the sauce and guacamole and the remaining ¼ cup cheddar cheese.

HERB-YOGURT CHICKEN

When I attended the rehearsal dinner for my friend Eric, we were served a chicken dish very similar to this one. I asked how to make it—and then because I am who I am, I added even more flavor by tossing in some dill and garlic. The yogurt-cucumber sauce acts as a wonderful cooling agent.

Serves 6

HERB-YOGURT-CUCUMBER SAUCE:

1½ cucumbers, peeled, seeded, and diced (about 1½ cups)
3 cups plain Greek-style yogurt
Juice of 2 lemons
3 tablespoons chopped fresh dill
2 tablespoons chopped garlic
Kosher salt and freshly ground black pepper

CHICKEN:

¾ cup extra-virgin olive oil
Juice of 3 lemons
6 cloves garlic, minced
Kosher salt and freshly ground black pepper
6 boneless chicken breast halves, with skin
6 cups spinach leaves, optional

TO MAKE THE SAUCE: Dice the cucumbers and put them in a large bowl. Stir in the yogurt, lemon juice, dill, and garlic. Season to taste with salt and pepper and stir well. Cover and refrigerate until ready to use but for no longer than 3 hours.

TO MAKE THE CHICKEN: In a glass, ceramic, or another nonreactive bowl, whisk together the oil, lemon juice, and garlic. Season to taste with salt and pepper.

Lay the chicken breasts in a shallow glass dish, skin side up, and pour the marinade over them. Cover and refrigerate for at least 30 minutes and up to 8 hours.

Prepare a medium-hot to hot fire in a charcoal or gas grill and oil the grill grates.

Preheat the oven to 350°F.

Lift the chicken from the marinade and grill, skin-side down, until the skin is nicely browned and is well marked with char lines, about 6 minutes. Turn and cook until the chicken is nearly cooked through and an instant-read thermometer inserted in the thickest part of the meat registers 145°F to 150°F, 6 to 7 minutes longer. Transfer the chicken to a small roasting pan and roast about 10 minutes, or until cooked through and the instant-read thermometer inserted in the thickest part of the meat registers 160°F.

Arrange the spinach, if using, on a serving platter. Slice the chicken into strips and arrange over the bed of spinach. Top with the yogurt sauce and serve.

CHEDDAR BISCUITS STUFFED WITH SAVORY BAKED EGGS

The key to making these tasty biscuits is to partially scramble the eggs before spooning them over the biscuits. If you pour raw eggs over them, the eggs won't set. I make these with store-bought biscuits, but if you are feeling ambitious, by all means make your own. In the McCargo family, we like these for supper and breakfast, and because they are trouble-free to eat, they are a favorite whenever we're lucky enough to have breakfast in bed! My kids love making these stuffed biscuits alongside me, and yours probably will, too.

Serves 6

8 slices bacon
12 unbaked store-bought cheddar-flavored biscuits
3 tablespoons unsalted butter
2 shallots, minced
2 tablespoons minced garlic
12 large eggs, beaten
1 tablespoon smoked paprika
2 cups grated cheddar cheese
½ tablespoon salt
1 tablespoon freshly ground black pepper
1 bunch fresh chives, chopped
About 3 cups Sweet Sausage Gravy (page 202)

TO PREPARE: Preheat the oven to 425°F.

Lay the bacon on a baking sheet and bake for 20 to 24 minutes, until crispy (for more on cooking bacon, see pages 58–59). Remove from the baking sheet and drain on paper towels. When cool enough to handle, crumble the bacon.

Meanwhile, spray a 12-cup muffin pan with flavorless vegetable cooking spray. Mold the biscuits to fit into each muffin cup without filling it and bake for about 8 minutes, or until the biscuits begin to brown and are baked about halfway through.

In a large nonstick skillet, melt the butter over medium-high heat. When hot, add the shallots and garlic and cook, stirring, until the shallots are translucent, 2 to 3 minutes. Add the eggs and paprika. Lower the heat to medium and cook, stirring frequently, for 2 to 4 minutes.

Remove the pan from the heat and stir in the crumbled bacon, cheese, salt, and pepper. Return to medium-high heat and cook for an additional 2 minutes. Mix in the chives, and when the eggs begin to coagulate but are still runny, ladle the eggs into each par-baked biscuit to fill. Return the muffin pan to the oven and bake for 5 to 6 minutes, until the eggs set. Remove and serve with the sausage gravy.

SLAMMIN' SPICY SALMON FRIED RICE

It's not typical to serve salmon with fried rice, but why not? This tastes great. I was inspired to create this dish when a buddy of mine named Jason, who was a cop in Camden, told me about some fantastic fried rice he had tried at an African restaurant in Philadelphia, which is just across the Delaware River from Camden. I never made it to the restaurant to sample the fried rice, but after listening to Jason describe the dish, I tried my hand at it. Here's the outcome. Jason likes this, although he says it's not too similar to the rice at the African restaurant.

Serves 6 to 8

Four 8-ounce boneless, skinless salmon fillets
1½ cups Asian Mustard Sauce (page 189)
3 tablespoons canola oil
4 large eggs, lightly beaten
1 tablespoon sesame oil
6 cups cooked white rice
1 cup bean sprouts
½ cup thinly sliced carrots
½ cup sliced scallions, white and green parts

TO PREPARE: Lay the salmon in a shallow glass, ceramic, or another nonreactive dish. Spread about ¼ cup of the mustard sauce over the salmon, turn the fillets, and spread another ½ cup of sauce on the other side. Cover and refrigerate for at least 4 hours and up to 6 hours.

Preheat the oven to 400°F.

Lay the fillets on a roasting rack set in a roasting pan and bake for about 20 minutes, or until cooked through. Remove from the oven, and when cool, flake the fillets into large pieces.

Meanwhile, in a nonstick skillet, heat 1 tablespoon of the oil over medium heat and scramble the eggs, stirring often, until firmly cooked.

In a large skillet, heat the remaining 2 tablespoons of canola oil over high heat. When hot, add the sesame oil and rice to the pan and cook, stirring vigorously, for 5 to 6 minutes. Add the bean sprouts, carrots, scallions, flaked salmon, and scrambled eggs. Toss gently, and then stir in the remaining ¾ cup mustard sauce. When heated through, serve.

MY FAVORITE SIDE DISHES

FOR SOME REASON THAT I DON'T WHOLLY UNDERSTAND, folks have trouble deciding on side dishes. "What goes with what?" they ask, as they might when wondering whether a silk scarf matches a pair of shoes. The truth of the matter is that there is only one hard-and-fast rule when it comes to pairing foods: Follow your palate. (Or to put it another way: Go with your gut!) Common sense says you wouldn't serve mashed potatoes and a cheesy pasta casserole at the same meal, but your eyes, your nose, and your taste buds tell you that those mashers would taste fantastic with a steak or pork chop. Just about any meat, poultry, or fish that's been grilled or pan-seared tastes great with a side of orzo (one of my faves), rice, or spuds. The same goes for greens such as spinach and kale. If you're serving pasta, stick with simple salads and maybe some cooked beans.

I don't offer a large number of sides here, but these are among my favorites. I love anything jazzed up with citrus or fresh herbs. I use turnips to sweeten creamed spinach, and I enrich simple orzo with heady sage, luxuriant prosciutto, and creamy fontina cheese. And I add crunch to peas and rice with the addition of bean sprouts. All are very, very good!

When New Jersey's farmers' markets are bursting with freshly harvested tomatoes, sweet corn, cucumbers, summer squash, and pole beans—and then later in the season with fall squashes, greens, potatoes, and turnips—I barely have to think about what to serve on the side. The vegetables speak for themselves because New Jersey is not called the Garden State by chance. Believe it or not, our farmed vegetables and fruits are among the best in the country. The challenge is to decide what to serve alongside all this glorious bounty. You won't go wrong with these beauties!

RECIPES

SWEET PEAS WITH BEAN SPROUTS

Anyone who has known me all my life might be surprised to see a recipe for peas in my book. When I was a kid, I avoided them at all costs. But I like them now, and I have a great partiality to bean sprouts. When the two are cooked like this, with a nice honey-sweetened pan sauce, the vegetables pop. This dish is best with fresh peas, but frozen work well, too. I don't recommend canned peas.

Serves 6

- **3 tablespoons unsalted butter**
- **3 tablespoons sliced scallions, white and green parts**
- **1½ tablespoons minced fresh ginger**
- **1½ tablespoons minced garlic**
- **1 pound shelled fresh peas or frozen peas**
- **1 cup bean sprouts**
- **Pinch of crushed red pepper flakes**
- **¼ cup chicken broth**
- **1½ tablespoons honey**
- **1½ tablespoons sesame oil**
- **Salt and freshly cracked black pepper**
- **3 tablespoons sesame seeds, optional**

TO PREPARE: In a large skillet, melt the butter over medium-high. When hot, add the scallions, ginger, and garlic and cook, stirring, until the vegetables begin to soften, about 2 minutes.

Add the peas, sprouts, and red pepper flakes and cook, stirring, until the sprouts soften a little, 2 to 3 minutes. Stir in the broth, honey, and sesame oil and season to taste with salt and pepper. Cook until the glaze is hot and the peas are nicely coated. Sprinkle with the sesame seeds, if desired, stir well, and serve.

CREAMED SPINACH AND TURNIP CASSEROLE

When I first started eating at the high-priced steak houses in New York and other cities, I was generally disappointed by the creamed spinach. I decided to add turnips to mine and suddenly had a dish to celebrate. The turnips have a nice firm texture and add sweetness that balances the flavors and textures.

Serves 10 to 12

1 pound turnips, peeled and cubed
1 quart chicken broth
½ cup diced Canadian bacon
¼ cup diced shallots
½ cup heavy cream
One 1-ounce envelope vegetable soup mix
1 cup Aaron's Easy Roux (page 203)
1 pound frozen chopped spinach, thawed and squeezed of excess moisture
1 cup panko bread crumbs
¼ cup (½ stick) unsalted butter, melted
¼ cup shredded parmesan cheese
¼ cup shredded smoked cheddar cheese
1½ teaspoons smoked paprika

TO PREPARE: Preheat the oven to 375°F.

In a large saucepan, put the turnips and broth, bring to a boil, and cook until very tender, 30 to 40 minutes. Drain the turnips, transfer to a bowl, and set aside.

Meanwhile, in a large skillet, cook the bacon with the shallots over medium heat, stirring, until the bacon is cooked and has rendered most of its fat and the shallots begin to caramelize, 8 to 10 minutes.

Stir the heavy cream and vegetable soup mix into the saucepan with the drained turnips and add this mixture to the skillet. Stir in the roux and spinach and cook, stirring frequently and watching carefully so the mixture does not scorch, for 15 to 20 minutes. Transfer to a greased 9-inch square glass baking dish.

In a small bowl, stir together the bread crumbs, butter, cheeses, and paprika. Spread the cheese mixture over the top of the casserole and bake for 15 to 20 minutes, until the cheese and bread crumbs are golden brown. Serve hot.

CABBAGE WITH KALE AND TOASTED PINE NUTS

This dish is all about my wife, Kim, who has always loved kale. When she was pregnant with our daughter, Jordan, she couldn't get enough of it, and I cooked it every which way. This is one of our favorites, wilted in a skillet with some pine nuts and cabbage. It always makes Kim happy.

Serves 10

- 1 pound kale, trimmed and chopped
- ½ cup pine nuts
- 1 tablespoon unsalted butter
- 1 tablespoon olive oil
- ½ cup diced onion
- Two 1-ounce envelopes vegetable soup mix
- 1 tablespoon granulated onion powder
- ½ tablespoon chopped fresh thyme leaves
- ½ teaspoon freshly ground black pepper
- 1 pound green or purple cabbage, cored and chopped

TO PREPARE: In a large pot or deep skillet, bring about 1 inch of water to a simmer. Cook the kale in the simmering water, tightly covered, until softened, 8 to 10 minutes. (Alternatively, steam the kale in a steamer over about 1 inch of simmering water until softened, about 10 minutes.) Drain and set aside.

Preheat the oven to 350°F. Spread the pine nuts on a rimmed baking sheet and toast for about 5 minutes, stirring them once during toasting; watch carefully so that they don't scorch. Set aside.

In a large skillet, heat the butter and olive oil over medium-high heat. When the butter melts, add the onion and cook, stirring, until it begins to caramelize, 5 to 6 minutes. Add the vegetable soup mix, onion powder, thyme, and pepper, and then stir in ¼ cup of water. (If you have ¼ cup of chicken or vegetable stock on hand, use it instead of water.)

Add the kale, stir so that it's incorporated, cover the skillet, and cook over medium heat, stirring every now and then, for 10 minutes. Stir in the cabbage, cover, raise the heat to medium-high, and cook, stirring occasionally, until the greens are wilted and cooked through, about 20 minutes longer. Stir in the toasted pine nuts and serve.

CHILLED TACO LOCO RICE

I went a little crazy when I developed this recipe. I wanted to use my taco blend with rice, and so here you have the result. I like this dish alongside Pork Empanadas with Ranchero Sauce (page 34), Savory Taco Chicken Pizza with Guacamole and Chipotle Salsa (page 46), or Blackened Cod with Blue Cheese Sauce (page 133). It would also add a lot of zip to a plain grilled or broiled chicken breast or steak.

Serves 6

3 cups jasmine rice (see Note, page 161)
One 15-ounce can black beans, drained
1 cup mild or spicy chunky salsa
One 4.5-ounce can diced green chiles in brine
¼ cup chopped scallions, white and green parts
2 tablespoons Taco Blend (page 192)
2 tablespoons chopped chipotle chile peppers in adobo sauce
2 tablespoons chopped fresh cilantro

TO PREPARE: Cook the rice according to the package directions.

In a large bowl, toss the cooked rice with the black beans, salsa, green chiles, scallions, taco blend, chipotle chile, and cilantro. Serve at room temperature.

IS THERE A DIFFERENCE BETWEEN CANNED BEANS AND DRIED BEANS?

These are the same food, with the only difference being that canned beans are ready to eat while dried beans need to be soaked for hours and then slowly simmered in water to cover until they soften. The slow cooking allows them to hydrate effectively and prevents them from splitting open. I call for canned beans in my recipes simply because they are convenient—and a very good product. But if you prefer to buy dried beans and cook them yourself, you will save money. If you cook a lot at a time, you can freeze the leftovers, and they'll be ready when you are.

Of course, I am talking about legumes here: black beans, navy beans, cannellini beans, kidney beans, and so forth. (I am not talking about fresh beans, which include string beans, haricot verts, and wax beans.) Other legumes, such as lentils and split peas, don't need to be soaked before they are cooked.

TOASTED JASMINE RICE WITH CRUNCHY BEAN SPROUTS

Since bean sprouts often are sold in 1-pound bags, I have tried to come up with a few recipes that use them. I love their crunch. I also like the gentle perfume of jasmine rice. When it's cooked properly, it does not turn mushy but stays nice and loose when mixed with the sprouts. I like this side with Jerk Me Sweet Pork Chops (page 134) or Blackened Cod with Blue Cheese Sauce (page 133).

Serves 4 to 6

3 tablespoons peanut oil
2 cups jasmine rice (see Note)
3 cups chicken broth
2 bunches whole scallions, trimmed
3 tablespoons olive oil
Salt and freshly cracked black pepper
1½ cups bean sprouts
1 cup coarsely chopped dried fruit, such as currants, cranberries, and raisins
3 tablespoons chopped fresh cilantro
2 red jalapeño chile peppers, minced
Juice of 1 lemon

TO PREPARE: Prepare a hot fire in a charcoal or gas grill and oil the grill grates.

In a large saucepan, heat the peanut oil over medium-high heat. When hot, add the rice and toast until fragrant, about 1 minute. Add the broth and bring to a boil. Lower the heat, cover, and simmer until the liquid is absorbed, 18 to 20 minutes. Remove from the heat and let sit, still covered, for about 10 minutes.

Toss the scallions with the olive oil and season to taste with salt and pepper. Grill, turning, until nicely charred on all sides, 1 to 2 minutes. Chop the scallions coarsely. Fold the scallions, bean sprouts, dried fruit, cilantro, jalapeños, and lemon juice into the rice and serve.

NOTE: While most of the packaged rice sold in today's markets does not require rinsing before it's cooked, I usually rinse jasmine rice to rid it of excess starch.

ORZO, WINTER SQUASH, AND APPLEWOOD-SMOKED BACON

This dish will keep you in the house on a blustery fall day. I don't usually go for comfort foods, not because I don't like them but because they are not generally as highly seasoned as I like, but this orzo is comfort food with a capital C. I love it with roasted chicken or pan-seared flounder. The cheeses make the orzo creamy, offset by the saltiness of the bacon and the sweetness of the squash.

Serves 6

- 2 cups peeled, cubed butternut squash (1 medium squash)
- 1 tablespoon olive oil
- 10 slices applewood-smoked bacon
- 2 tablespoons diced shallots
- ¼ cup chopped scallions, white and green parts
- 1 tablespoon chopped fresh basil leaves
- 1 teaspoon freshly ground black pepper
- ½ teaspoon kosher salt
- 1 pound orzo
- ½ cup chicken broth
- ½ cup mascarpone cheese
- ¼ cup shredded parmesan cheese
- 2 tablespoons chopped fresh flat-leaf parsley leaves

TO PREPARE: Preheat the oven to 350°F.

In a large roasting pan, toss the cubed squash with the olive oil and roast for 30 to 35 minutes, until fork-tender. Remove from the oven and set aside.

In a large, deep skillet, cook the bacon until crisp. Drain on paper towels and discard all but 2 tablespoons of the rendered fat in the skillet. Add the shallots to the skillet and cook over medium-high heat, stirring, until they begin to brown, 2 to 3 minutes. Add the squash, scallions, basil, pepper, and salt and cook over medium heat, stirring, until hot and well mixed.

Meanwhile, in a saucepan, cook the orzo according to the package directions.

Add the orzo and broth to the skillet and cook until heated through, 5 to 7 minutes. Remove from the heat and crumble the bacon into the skillet. Add the mascarpone and stir.

In a small bowl, toss the parmesan with the parsley. Sprinkle the parmesan-parsley mixture over each serving.

LEMON-PEPPER ORZO

I call this the "poor man's risotto" because it's just as smooth, creamy, and seductive as that famed rice dish. I made this for *The Next Food Network Star* competition, and clearly it passed muster with the judges. Orzo is easy to find, inexpensive, cooks more quickly than rice, and yet has a similar texture. I find this dish deliciously refreshing. What more is there to say?

Serves 6

3¼ cups chicken broth
1½ cups orzo
½ cup heavy cream
½ cup grated parmesan cheese
Juice of 3 lemons
3 tablespoons mascarpone cheese
3 tablespoons unsalted butter
3 tablespoons chopped fresh chives
1½ tablespoons freshly ground black pepper
1½ teaspoons grated lemon zest
Kosher salt

TO PREPARE: In a medium saucepan, bring the broth to a boil over high heat. Add the orzo and cook until the liquid is almost absorbed and the orzo is tender, 8 to 10 minutes. Turn off the heat.

Stir the heavy cream, parmesan, lemon juice, mascarpone, butter, chives, pepper, and lemon zest into the hot pasta. Season to taste with salt, if necessary, and serve.

AARON'S MASHED POTATOES

I like to make mashed potatoes with Yukon Golds, tender, yellow-tinged potatoes with a pleasing sweetness that greets the butter, milk, and cream with nothing but joy. Of course, red- or white-skinned all-purpose potatoes work well, too. I would stay away from russets, which are better baked. As far as what to serve this with? You name it! (Although I wouldn't suggest pasta or rice.)

Serves 6

6 Yukon Gold potatoes, peeled and cut into 1-inch cubes (about 6 cups)
1 cup heavy cream
1 cup milk
½ cup (1 stick) unsalted butter
2 teaspoons salt
1 teaspoon freshly ground black pepper

TO PREPARE: In a medium saucepan, put the potatoes and add enough cold water to cover by about 1 inch. Bring to a boil over high heat and cook until fork-tender, about 20 minutes. Drain the potatoes and return to the pan.

Meanwhile, in another saucepan, heat the heavy cream, milk, and butter over medium-high heat until hot. Pour the cream mixture over the potatoes and, using a potato masher or fork, mash the potatoes until slightly chunky. Add the salt and pepper and serve.

IS THERE MUCH DIFFERENCE AMONG POTATOES?

Who doesn't like potatoes? And yes, there are a few things to know about selecting them. Russet potatoes, also called baking or Idaho potatoes, are best for baking. Thin-skinned all-purpose potatoes—also known as red or white potatoes—are best for boiling and mashing. I like Yukon Gold potatoes, which have a yellow tint and very thin skin, for mashed potatoes because they are tender and have a slightly buttery flavor. New potatoes are immature all-purpose potatoes and are deliciously sweet, perfect for roasting and grilling. Fingerling potatoes are small, narrow, knobby white potatoes that can be cooked in the same ways as new potatoes.

CHEESY POTATOES WITH BACON AND OREGANO

I never liked scalloped potatoes when I was growing up, and I suspect it was because they came from a box. I wanted to come up with a cheesy potato dish that tasted really, really good. Here is my solution, and it is so easy that you will never be tempted to cook potatoes from a box again (please!). I serve these with steak or lamb, and my kids like them with fish sticks.

Serves 8 to 10

- 3 quarts canola oil
- 2 pounds fingerling potatoes, quartered or halved to produce even-size pieces about the size of walnuts
- 10 slices bacon, cooked until crispy and crumbled
- 1 cup shredded cheddar cheese
- 1 cup shredded Gouda cheese
- 1½ cups barbecue sauce
- 2 teaspoons fresh oregano leaves
- 1 teaspoon freshly ground black pepper

TO PREPARE: Preheat the oven to 400°F. Grease a 9-inch square glass baking dish.

In a large, heavy pot, heat the oil over high heat until a deep-fat thermometer reaches a temperature of 375°F. Using a slotted spoon or tongs and without crowding the pot, submerge the potatoes in the oil and fry until golden brown, 4 to 6 minutes. Lift the potatoes from the oil and drain on paper towels. Let the oil return to 350°F between batches.

In a large bowl, mix together the bacon, cheeses, barbecue sauce, oregano, and pepper. Add the potatoes to the mixture and stir until incorporated. Transfer the mixture to the prepared dish and bake for about 15 minutes, or until hot and bubbling. Serve hot.

ROSEMARY-MASHED YUKON GOLD POTATOES

The secret to really good mashed potatoes is to start with Yukon Gold potatoes. I think they are superior to russet or red bliss, and so whenever I can, I use them for mashers. The rosemary is a nice addition, and a little goes a long way, as you will discover. For more traditional mashed potatoes, just omit the rosemary.

Serves 6

- 6 Yukon Gold potatoes, peeled and cut into 1-inch cubes (about 6 cups)
- 1 cup heavy cream
- 1 cup milk
- ½ cup (1 stick) unsalted butter
- 2 tablespoons fresh rosemary leaves
- 2 teaspoons salt
- 1 teaspoon freshly ground black pepper

TO PREPARE: In a medium saucepan, put the potatoes and add enough cold water to cover by about 1 inch. Bring to a boil over high heat and cook until fork-tender, about 20 minutes. Drain the potatoes and return to the pan.

Meanwhile, in another saucepan, heat the heavy cream, milk, butter, and rosemary over medium-high heat until hot. Pour the cream mixture over the potatoes and, using a potato masher or fork, mash the potatoes until slightly chunky. Add the salt and pepper, and serve.

SAVORY SAGE, PROSCIUTTO, AND FONTINA ORZO

I am extremely fond of orzo, the pasta with the consistency and appearance of rice. With savory sage, creamy fontina and mascarpone, and fatty prosciutto, this dish has an outstanding flavor profile with a pleasing texture to match. If you want this to be vegetarian, use vegetable broth instead of chicken broth and substitute mushrooms or asparagus for the prosciutto.

Serves 6

3 tablespoons unsalted butter
½ cup diced prosciutto
2 shallots, diced
3 fresh sage leaves, finely chopped
3¼ cups chicken broth
1½ cups orzo
½ cup heavy cream
½ cup shredded fontina cheese
3 tablespoons mascarpone cheese
3 tablespoons chopped fresh chives
1½ tablespoons freshly cracked black pepper, plus more if necessary
Salt

TO PREPARE: In a small skillet, melt the butter over medium-high heat. When the butter melts, add the prosciutto, shallots, and sage and cook, stirring, until the shallots begin to brown, 3 to 4 minutes. Remove the skillet from the heat and set aside.

Meanwhile, in a medium saucepan, bring the broth to a boil over high heat. Add the orzo and cook until the liquid is nearly absorbed and the orzo is tender, 8 to 10 minutes. Remove the pan from the heat and stir in the heavy cream, cheeses, chives, pepper, and prosciutto mixture. Season with more salt and pepper, if necessary. Serve hot.

DRESSINGS, MAYONNAISES, SPICE BLENDS, SAUCES, & CONDIMENTS

THE RECIPES IN THIS CHAPTER ARE MY ARSENAL, the tools I use to punch up other ingredients, so that the final dish shouts with flavor. Big, bold flavors: that's what I am about, that's what I love, that's what I strive for whenever I walk in a kitchen. I hope you'll embrace this philosophy and that every time you cook, you'll kick it up just a little. It's so easy to sprinkle seasoning blend on chicken, pork, or fish; it takes minutes to stir together your own salad dressing; there's very little effort to stirring some herbs and spices into mayonnaise. And when you take the extra steps, your food is zestier and more exciting—and your family and friends will notice.

With the exception of the salad dressings, I use all these recipes in at least one dish in the book, and my hope is that you will take your cue from me and experiment with swapping out a seasoning mix or mayonnaise for another to please your own taste buds. Rub the seasonings into the meat and let it marinate in its own juices for a few hours in the refrigerator. Allow it to come to room temperature, and then cook as planned. The flavors will pop! I make the spice blends in fairly large quantities and keep them in zip-top plastic bags.

Toss side salads with the vinaigrettes, or use them to marinate chicken, fish, pork, or beef. (If you use them to marinate seafood, don't marinate it for longer than an hour or so to prevent the food from turning mushy.) When you make the Warm Cider Vinegar, Dijon, and Bacon Dressing (page 176), pour it over sturdy greens such as romaine, arugula, or spinach just before serving so that they just begin to wilt. I make the salad dressings in large amounts and keep them in jars. They taste so much better than store-bought and don't cost as much either. I do the same with the mayonnaises, which will keep for several days.

RECIPES

BASIL-BALSAMIC VINAIGRETTE

Makes about 4 cups

- 2 large egg yolks (see Note below)
- 1 cup balsamic vinegar
- 2 cups canola oil
- ½ cup olive oil
- 1 cup packed fresh basil leaves
- ¼ cup sugar
- 2 tablespoons salt
- 1½ teaspoons freshly ground black pepper
- 1 teaspoon crushed red pepper flakes

TO PREPARE: In a blender, mix the egg yolks with the vinegar on high speed until well blended and frothy, about 2 minutes. With the motor running, add the canola oil in a slow, steady stream. Once the canola oil is incorporated, slowly add the olive oil.

Add the basil, sugar, salt, pepper, and red pepper flakes and blend until the vinaigrette is well mixed, about 30 seconds longer. Use right away, or refrigerate for up to 2 weeks. Blend for about 1 minute or shake to mix before using.

NOTE: To ensure this dressing is as smooth, creamy and rich as possible, I rely on a couple of egg yolks. Some folks are anxious about eating raw eggs and I share their concern. Make sure the grade A eggs have been refrigerated, the shells are clean, and avoid mixing the yolks with pieces of shell when you separate the eggs. Small kids, the elderly, and anyone with a compromised immune system should avoid any raw animal products.

LEMON VINAIGRETTE

Makes about 3 cups

1 large egg yolk (see Note, page 173)
1 cup fresh lemon juice (about 6 to 8 lemons)
2 cups canola oil
½ cup olive oil
¼ cup chopped shallots
¼ cup chopped fresh cilantro leaves
2 tablespoons salt
2 teaspoons lemon-pepper seasoning
1 teaspoon freshly ground black pepper

TO PREPARE: In a blender, mix the egg yolk with the lemon juice on high speed until well blended and frothy, about 2 minutes. With the motor running, add the canola oil in a slow, steady stream. Once the canola oil is incorporated, slowly add the olive oil.

Add the shallots, cilantro, salt, lemon-pepper, and black pepper and blend until the vinaigrette is well mixed, about 30 seconds longer. Use right away, or refrigerate for up to 2 weeks. Blend for about 1 minute or shake to mix before using.

MINTED LIME VINAIGRETTE

Makes about 2 cups

½ cup fresh lime juice (4 to 5 limes)
¾ cup canola oil
¼ cup olive oil
2 tablespoons diced shallots
2 tablespoons chopped fresh mint leaves
1 tablespoon grated lime zest
Salt and freshly ground black pepper

TO PREPARE: Pour the lime juice into a blender. With the blender on medium speed, slowly add the canola oil to the blender. Increase the speed to high and slowly add the olive oil. Add the shallots, mint, and lime zest and pulse to mix. Season to taste with salt and pepper and pulse several times until the vinaigrette is blended. Use right away, or cover and refrigerate for up to 2 weeks. Whisk or shake before using.

WARM CIDER VINEGAR, DIJON, AND BACON DRESSING

Makes about 2 cups

6 to 8 slices bacon
½ cup finely diced onion
1 cup cider vinegar
1 cup Dijon mustard
1 cup packed dark brown sugar
1 teaspoon salt
1 teaspoon freshly ground black pepper
¼ cup chopped scallions, white and green parts

TO PREPARE: In a large skillet, cook the bacon over medium heat until crispy. Remove the bacon from the skillet and drain on paper towels, reserving the fat in the skillet. When the bacon is cool, crumble it into pieces. Add the onion to the skillet with the bacon fat and cook, stirring, until lightly caramelized, 4 to 5 minutes. Stir in the vinegar, mustard, and brown sugar and mix well. Season with the salt and pepper and cook until the dressing boils. Remove from the heat, let cool slightly, and stir in the bacon and scallions. Pour over sturdy greens, scattered with the bacon, while still hot, to wilt them.

THOUSAND ISLAND DRESSING

Makes about 1 cup

½ cup mayonnaise
¼ cup ketchup
¼ cup finely chopped dill pickles
1 tablespoon Worcestershire sauce
1 tablespoon chopped garlic
1 teaspoon fresh lemon juice
1 teaspoon salt

TO PREPARE: In a small bowl, stir together the mayonnaise, ketchup, pickles, Worcestershire sauce, garlic, lemon juice, and salt. Taste and adjust the seasoning, if necessary.

SWEET AND STICKY HONEY-SCALLION DIPPING SAUCE

Makes about 1½ cups

1 cup sour cream or low-fat Greek-style plain yogurt, drained

¼ cup honey

¼ cup chopped scallions, white and green parts

1 teaspoon cayenne pepper

Salt and freshly ground black pepper

TO PREPARE: In a small bowl, combine the sour cream, honey, scallions, and cayenne. Season to taste with salt and pepper. Cover and refrigerate for at least 1 hour to chill, or for up to 1 week. Stir before using.

ROASTED GARLIC MAYONNAISE

Makes about ¾ cup

1 cup mayonnaise
2 tablespoons chopped roasted garlic (see Note)
¼ teaspoon fresh lemon juice
¼ teaspoon finely grated lemon zest
¼ teaspoon kosher salt
¼ teaspoon coarsely ground black pepper

TO PREPARE: In a small bowl, mix together the mayonnaise, garlic, lemon juice, lemon zest, salt, and pepper until well incorporated. Use right away, or cover and refrigerate for up to 5 days.

NOTE: To roast garlic, peel the papery outer layers of skin from a whole head of garlic. Do not separate the individual cloves. Using a large, sharp knife, cut the top off the head of garlic to expose the tops of the cloves. Put the head in a small baking dish and rub it with a good amount of olive oil. The exposed end of the head of garlic should be facing up. Cover the dish with aluminum foil and roast in a preheated 350°F oven for about 30 minutes, or until the cloves are soft. (Alternatively, wrap the olive oil-rubbed garlic head in aluminum foil for roasting.)

Let the head cool so that it's easy to handle. Pull the cloves from the head—they will separate easily—and squeeze the soft flesh from the skins. The garlic is now ready to use.

LEMON-PEPPER-GARLIC MAYONNAISE

Makes about 1¼ cups

1 cup mayonnaise

2 tablespoons fresh lemon juice

1 tablespoon chopped garlic

1 tablespoon chopped fresh cilantro leaves

1½ teaspoons lemon-pepper seasoning

TO PREPARE: In a small bowl, stir together the mayonnaise and lemon juice. Stir in the garlic, cilantro, and lemon-pepper seasoning. Serve right away, or cover and refrigerate for up to 5 days.

ARUGULA MAYONNAISE

Makes about 2 cups

1 cup mayonnaise
2 teaspoons fresh lemon juice
2 tablespoons Worcestershire sauce
1½ cups finely chopped arugula
2 tablespoons finely chopped garlic
Salt and freshly ground black pepper
Dash of hot pepper sauce, such as Tabasco

TO PREPARE: In a small bowl, stir together the mayonnaise, lemon juice, and Worcestershire sauce. Stir in the arugula and garlic and season to taste with salt, pepper, and hot pepper sauce. Serve right away, or cover and refrigerate for up to 5 days.

DILL MAYONNAISE

Makes about 1¼ cups

1 cup mayonnaise
2 tablespoons fresh lemon juice
1 tablespoon chopped fresh dill
2 teaspoons finely chopped shallots
1 teaspoon lemon-pepper seasoning
Salt and freshly ground black pepper

TO PREPARE: In a small bowl, stir together the mayonnaise and lemon juice. Stir in the dill, shallots, and lemon-pepper seasoning. Season to taste with salt and pepper. Serve right away, or cover and refrigerate for up to 5 days.

CILANTRO MAYONNAISE

Makes about 3 cups

2 cups mayonnaise
½ cup fresh lemon juice (3 to 4 lemons)
½ cup chopped fresh cilantro leaves
2 tablespoons diced shallots
1 tablespoon lemon-pepper seasoning
½ teaspoon dried red pepper flakes
Dash of Worcestershire sauce

TO PREPARE: In a medium bowl, stir together the mayonnaise, lemon juice, cilantro, shallots, lemon-pepper seasoning, red pepper flakes, and Worcestershire sauce. Cover and refrigerate for at least 20 minutes to give the mayonnaise time to set, or refrigerate for up to 5 days.

WHAT ARE CHIPOTLE PEPPERS?

Chipotle peppers are smoked jalapeños packed in a mildly spicy, tomato-based sauce called adobo sauce. They are generally sold in cans. When you use them, mix the chopped peppers with a little of the adobo sauce to bolster the flavor. Chipotles are hot, and their strength develops as they sit in the cooked dish. If you decide to double a recipe, don't double the number of chipotles until you have tasted the finished dish. Then, if you like, increase the chipotles next time you make it.

CHIPOTLE MAYONNAISE

Makes about 1¼ cups

1 cup mayonnaise
¼ cup fresh lemon juice
4 chipotle chile peppers in adobo sauce, minced
1 tablespoon chopped fresh flat-leaf parsley
1 tablespoon finely chopped garlic
1 teaspoon salt
1 teaspoon freshly ground black pepper

TO PREPARE: In a small bowl, stir together the mayonnaise, lemon juice, chipotle chiles, parsley, and garlic. Add the salt and pepper and mix well. Taste and adjust the seasoning, if necessary. Serve right away, or cover and refrigerate for up to 5 days.

PESTO MAYONNAISE

Makes about 1½ cups

1 cup mayonnaise

2 tablespoons fresh lemon juice

¼ cup chopped fresh basil leaves

1 tablespoon chopped garlic

1 tablespoon Worcestershire sauce

Salt and freshly ground black pepper

TO PREPARE: In a small bowl, stir together the mayonnaise and lemon juice. Stir in the basil, garlic, and Worcestershire. Season to taste with salt and pepper. Serve right away, or cover and refrigerate for up to 5 days.

DIJON MUSTARD–GRUYÈRE CHEESE SAUCE

Makes about 2 cups

2 tablespoons olive oil
2 shallots, minced
2 teaspoons salt
2 teaspoons freshly ground black pepper
1½ tablespoons all-purpose flour
⅔ cup heavy cream
3 teaspoons chicken bouillon powder
1 cup shredded Gruyère or Swiss cheese
¼ cup Dijon mustard
1 teaspoon smoked paprika
2 tablespoons chopped fresh flat-leaf parsley

TO PREPARE: In a small saucepan, heat the oil over medium heat. When hot, add the shallots, salt, and pepper and cook, stirring, until the shallots are softened, about 4 minutes. Sprinkle the flour over the shallots and stir until smooth and thickened. Reduce the heat and add the heavy cream and bouillon powder, whisking to blend. Stir in the cheese and cook, stirring, until melted.

Decrease the heat to low, add the mustard and paprika, and whisk well. When heated through, stir in the parsley and serve.

HORSERADISH MUSTARD

Makes about 1 cup

- 1/4 cup whole-grain mustard
- 1/4 cup Dijon mustard
- 1/4 cup prepared hot horseradish cream
- 2 tablespoons freshly grated horseradish
- 1 tablespoon minced fresh cilantro leaves
- Salt and freshly ground black pepper

TO PREPARE: In a small bowl, stir together the mustards and horseradish cream. Stir in the grated horseradish and cilantro and season to taste with salt and pepper. Use right away, or cover and refrigerate for up to 2 weeks.

ASIAN MUSTARD SAUCE

Makes about 2 cups

1 cup soy sauce
¼ cup dry mustard
¼ cup rice wine vinegar
1 cup canola oil
¼ cup hot sesame oil
¼ cup chopped scallions, white and green parts
½ teaspoon crushed red pepper flakes

TO PREPARE: In a blender, put the soy sauce, dry mustard, and vinegar and pulse several times until mixed. With the motor running, slowly add the canola oil and sesame oil until blended. Add the scallions and red pepper flakes and pulse until well mixed, about 30 seconds. Use right away, or cover and refrigerate for up to 5 days.

CHESAPEAKE SPICE BLEND

Makes about ¼ cup

1 tablespoons Old Bay seasoning
1 tablespoon salt
1 teaspoon freshly ground black pepper
1 teaspoon cayenne pepper
1 teaspoon dried thyme
1 teaspoon granulated onion powder
1 teaspoon granulated garlic powder
½ teaspoon paprika

TO PREPARE: In a small bowl, stir together the Old Bay seasoning, salt, black pepper, cayenne, thyme, onion powder, garlic powder, and paprika. Taste and adjust the seasoning, if necessary. Store the seasoning in a lidded glass container or zipped plastic bag in a cool, dark place for up to 1 month.

DIG IT SPICE BLEND

Makes about ½ cup

2 tablespoons salt
1 tablespoon paprika
1 tablespoon granulated onion powder
1 tablespoon granulated garlic powder
1 tablespoon freshly ground black pepper
1 teaspoon seasoned salt

TO PREPARE: In a small bowl, stir together the salt, paprika, onion powder, garlic powder, pepper, and seasoned salt. Taste and adjust the seasoning, if necessary. Store the seasoning in a lidded glass container or zipped plastic bag in a cool, dark place for up to 1 month.

TACO BLEND

Makes about ⅓ cup

2 teaspoons salt
1 teaspoon chili powder
1 teaspoon dried oregano
1 teaspoon ground cumin
1 teaspoon cayenne pepper
1 teaspoon freshly ground black pepper
1 teaspoon granulated garlic powder
1 teaspoon granulated onion powder

TO PREPARE: In a small bowl, stir together the salt, chili powder, oregano, cumin, cayenne, black pepper, garlic powder, and onion powder. Taste and adjust the seasoning, if needed. Store the seasoning in a lidded glass container or zipped plastic bag in a cool, dark place for up to 1 month.

ITALIAN HERB BLEND

Makes about ½ cup

1 tablespoon dried basil
1 tablespoon dried oregano
1 tablespoon salt
2 teaspoons dried thyme
2 teaspoons dried marjoram
1 teaspoon freshly ground black pepper

TO PREPARE: In a small bowl, stir together the basil, oregano, salt, thyme, marjoram and pepper. Store the seasoning in a lidded glass container or zipped plastic bag in a cool, dark place for up to 1 month.

JERK SEASONING

Makes about ½ cup

- 2 tablespoons brown sugar
- 2½ teaspoons salt
- 2 teaspoons allspice
- 1 teaspoon cayenne pepper
- 1 teaspoon freshly ground black pepper
- 1 teaspoon granulated onion powder
- ½ teaspoon ground cinnamon
- ½ teaspoon granulated garlic powder
- ¼ teaspoon ground cumin
- ¼ teaspoon dried thyme

TO PREPARE: In a small bowl, stir together the brown sugar, salt, allspice, cayenne, black pepper, onion powder, cinnamon, garlic powder, cumin, and thyme. Store the seasoning in a lidded glass container or zipped plastic bag in a cool, dark place for up to 1 month.

MEAT SEASONING

Makes about 1/4 cup

- 2 tablespoons freshly ground black pepper
- 1 tablespoon salt
- 1 teaspoon ground cinnamon
- 1/2 teaspoon paprika
- 1/2 teaspoon dried thyme
- 1/2 teaspoon granulated onion powder
- 1/2 teaspoon granulated garlic powder
- 1/4 teaspoon ground cumin

TO PREPARE: In a small bowl, stir together the pepper, salt, cinnamon, paprika, thyme, onion powder, garlic powder, and cumin. Store the seasoning in a lidded glass container or zipped plastic bag in a cool, dark place for up to 1 month.

MOJO MARINADE

Makes about 3 cups

½ onion, coarsely chopped
1 cup orange juice, preferably freshly squeezed
½ cup lemon juice, preferably freshly squeezed
6 cloves garlic, peeled
2 tablespoons chopped fresh cilantro leaves
1½ tablespoons salt
1 tablespoon honey
1 tablespoon Jerk Seasoning (page 194)
1 tablespoon freshly ground black pepper
1 teaspoon dried oregano

TO PREPARE: In the bowl of a food processor fitted with the metal blade, put the onion, orange juice, lemon juice, garlic, cilantro, salt, honey, jerk seasoning, pepper, and oregano and pulse until smooth. Use right away or transfer to a lidded glass container and refrigerate for up to 1 month.

MARINATED SUN-DRIED TOMATOES

Makes about 1 cup

One 8-ounce jar oil-packed sun-dried tomatoes
2 tablespoons red wine vinegar
2 tablespoons sugar
1 tablespoon chopped garlic
1 teaspoon crushed red pepper flakes
Salt and freshly ground black pepper

TO PREPARE: In the bowl of a food processor fitted with the metal blade, put the sun-dried tomatoes and their oil, the vinegar, sugar, garlic, and red pepper flakes and pulse until coarsely chopped. Season to taste with salt and pepper. Use right away, or cover and refrigerate for up to 6 weeks.

ZESTY GUACAMOLE

Makes about 1 cup

2 ripe avocados, pitted, peeled, and diced
Juice of 2 limes
Grated zest of 1 lime
2 tablespoons chopped fresh cilantro leaves
2 tablespoons chopped scallions, white and green parts
1 tablespoon chopped garlic
1 tablespoon chili powder
1 tablespoon dried oregano
1 teaspoon cayenne pepper
1 teaspoon cumin
1 teaspoon salt
1 teaspoon freshly ground black pepper

TO PREPARE: In a small bowl, stir together the avocados, lime juice, lime zest, cilantro, scallions, and garlic. Add the chili powder, oregano, cayenne, and cumin and stir well, mashing the avocado slightly as you do. Season with the salt and pepper, taste, adjust the seasoning if necessary, and serve.

CHIPOTLE SALSA

Makes about 2 cups

- 4 to 6 plum tomatoes, cored, seeded, and finely diced
- ¼ cup chopped scallions, white and green parts
- ¼ cup finely diced red onion
- 2 to 3 chipotle chile peppers in adobo sauce, finely chopped
- 2 tablespoons honey
- Juice of 1 lime
- Salt and freshly ground black pepper

TO PREPARE: In a small bowl, stir together the tomatoes, scallions, onion, chipotle chiles and adobo sauce, honey, and lime juice. Season to taste with salt and pepper. Serve right away, or cover and refrigerate for up to 4 days.

EASY MARINARA SAUCE

Makes 1 quart

3 tablespoons olive oil
½ cup diced onion
1 tablespoon minced garlic
1 tablespoon crushed red pepper flakes
One 28-ounce can crushed tomatoes
1 tablespoon Italian Herb Blend (page 193)
1 tablespoon finely chopped fresh basil
1 tablespoon finely chopped fresh oregano
1½ teaspoons salt
1 teaspoon freshly ground black pepper

TO PREPARE: In a large skillet, heat the oil over medium-high heat. When hot, add the onions, garlic and red pepper flakes and cook, stirring to prevent burning, until the garlic is lightly browned, 1 to 2 minutes. Add the tomatoes, herb blend, basil, oregano, salt and pepper. Cover, lower the heat to medium, and simmer to give the flavors time to blend and the sauce to heat through, about 15 minutes. The sauce can be cooled and refrigerated for up to 3 days and frozen for up to 1 month.

TWO-IN-ONE SAUSAGE GRAVY

Makes about 3½ cups

One 6-ounce package chicken-flavored bread stuffing or your favorite stuffing mix
2 tablespoons chopped scallions, white and green parts
1 tablespoon chopped fresh flat-leaf parsley, plus more for garnish, optional
1 tablespoon chopped fresh thyme
8 ounces uncooked spicy Italian-style sausage (I like Bob Evans and also like to buy it in bulk; links, with casings removed, are okay, too.)
2¼ cups canola oil
1 cup all-purpose flour
3¼ cups chicken broth
2 tablespoons chicken bouillon powder

TO PREPARE: Prepare the stuffing according to the package instructions. Allow to cool to room temperature, and then stir the scallions, parsley, and thyme into the stuffing. Spread in a shallow pan and refrigerate for at least 1 hour, or until chilled. The stuffing can be made up to 24 hours ahead of time.

Pinch off small pieces of the sausage and roll into balls between dampened palms. You should have about 20 sausage balls. In a medium skillet over medium-high heat, cook the sausage balls, stirring occasionally so they brown evenly, until golden brown, 12 to 15 minutes. Transfer the cooked sausage balls to a plate.

Pour ¼ cup of the oil into the skillet and stir in ½ cup of the flour. Cook, stirring, until the mixture is smooth and well blended, 3 to 4 minutes. Add the broth and bouillon powder and stir to mix. Bring to a simmer and cook, stirring frequently, until the gravy thickens, 6 to 8 minutes. Cover and set aside to keep warm.

Using quarter-size disks of the stuffing (flatten balls of stuffing with your fingers), wrap the sausage balls in the stuffing. As each wrapped ball is made, put it on a plate. Make sure the sausage balls are completely enclosed by the stuffing. Spread the remaining ½ cup of flour in a shallow dish and roll the sausage-stuffing balls in it just to dust with flour.

Meanwhile, in a large saucepan, heat the remaining 2 cups of oil over medium-high heat until a deep-fat thermometer reaches a temperature of 350°F. Using a long-handled slotted spoon, carefully lower the a few sausage-stuffing balls at a time into the hot oil and cook until golden brown, 2 to 3 minutes, turning the balls in the oil to ensure even browning. Do not crowd the pan. Lift the balls from the oil with the slotted spoon and transfer to a large plate or baking sheet lined with paper towels to drain. Let the oil return to 350°F between batches. Put the sausage balls in the reserved gravy. Stir gently and heat over medium heat until warmed through. Serve garnished with fresh parsley, if desired.

SWEET SAUSAGE GRAVY

Makes about 4 cups

4 tablespoons (½ stick) unsalted butter
½ pound uncooked sweet Italian bulk sausage
½ medium onion, finely chopped
½ medium red bell pepper, seeded and finely chopped
1 tablespoon finely minced garlic
1 tablespoon crushed red pepper flakes
⅓ cup all-purpose flour
4 cups milk
Juice of 1 lemon
Salt and freshly ground black pepper
¼ cup grated parmesan cheese
3 tablespoons chopped fresh flat-leaf parsley

TO PREPARE: In a medium saucepan, melt the butter over medium-high heat. Add the sausage and cook it, breaking it apart with a wooden spoon, until nearly cooked through and thoroughly broken up, 8 to 10 minutes. Add the onion, bell pepper, garlic, and red pepper flakes and cook, stirring, until the mixture is soft and fragrant, about 3 minutes. Sprinkle the flour over the mixture and stir until the flour is absorbed.

Add the milk and cook, stirring, to break up any lumps in the flour and keep the sausage from burning. When the milk simmers, cook, stirring, until the gravy boils. Stir in the lemon juice and season to taste with salt and pepper. Cook for several minutes longer, stirring, until the gravy thickens. Stir in the cheese and parsley and serve.

SRIRACHA-HONEY BUTTER

Makes about 1¼ cups

1 cup (2 sticks) unsalted butter, softened
¼ cup honey
¼ cup chopped scallions, white and green parts
1 tablespoon Sriracha or another hot chile sauce
Salt and freshly ground black pepper

TO PREPARE: In a medium bowl, mash the butter with the honey, scallions, and Sriracha. Season to taste with salt and pepper. Lay a large piece of plastic wrap on a work surface and put the butter near one end. Roll the butter in the plastic wrap, using your fingers to form a log. Twist the ends of the plastic wrap to seal the packet and refrigerate for at least 2 hours or until chilled, or for up to 1 month.

AARON'S EASY ROUX

Makes about 1½ cups

1 cup all-purpose flour
¾ cup canola oil

TO PREPARE: In a medium bowl, stir the flour and oil together until smooth. You can double or triple the ingredients for the roux according to your needs.

INDULGENT DESSERTS & SWEET TREATS

WHEN IT'S TIME TO COME UP WITH DESSERT, I AM A HAPPY MAN. By their very nature, desserts lend themselves to indulgent excess—an area where I excel! I am not a pastry chef or a trained chocolatier, so my desserts are nothing if not approachable for most home cooks. I start with things everyone loves—cookies, cupcakes, and puddings—and take it from there.

I make use of cake mixes and I don't shy away from store-bought ice cream and easy-to-make sauces. Classic puddings such as bread pudding, rice pudding (made with orzo in the McCargo house), and even a simple white chocolate pudding are part of my repertoire, and I make a straightforward fruit cobbler that just about hollers "Fall is here!"

I jack up my desserts with candy bars, sweetened whipped cream, mascarpone cheese (can't get enough of it!), fresh fruit, and even spices, as in the Spicy Chocolate-Cherry Truffles on page 220. Nothing is too much for dessert, as long as you're true to the flavors and original intent of the dish.

I say, end the meal on a high note! Why hold back?

RECIPES

CANDY BAR COOKIES

These cookies are totally indulgent and lusciously gooey— pretty typical of the sort of cookies I like! When I was unemployed for a short time years ago, I toyed with the idea of starting a cookie business, and every recipe I came up with had a candy bar theme. Guess that tells you something about my inclinations! I have never lost my affection for cookies baked with pieces of candy bars. For these cookies, I like TAKE 5 bars, but you could substitute your favorite candy bar.

Makes about 40 cookies

1 cup (2 sticks) unsalted butter, softened
1 cup chunky peanut butter
1 cup sugar
½ cup packed light brown sugar
½ cup packed dark brown sugar
1½ teaspoons pure vanilla extract
2 large eggs
3 cups all-purpose flour
1 teaspoon baking soda
1 teaspoon baking powder
Pinch of salt
20 mini candy bars (I like TAKE 5 bars), halved

TO PREPARE: Preheat the oven to 350°F.

In the bowl of a standing mixer fitted with the paddle attachment and set on medium-high speed, cream together the butter, peanut butter, sugars, and vanilla for 3 to 5 minutes, until light and fluffy. With the mixer running at medium speed, add the eggs, 1 at a time, and mix until well incorporated.

In a large bowl, whisk together the flour, baking soda, baking powder, and salt until well combined. With the mixer on low speed, slowly add the flour mixture to the batter and beat just until blended. There should be no white streaks in the batter.

Using your hands, shape a heaping tablespoon of dough around each candy bar half. Smooth the batter around the bars into balls and make sure the candy bars are completely covered.

Put the balls of dough 3 to 4 inches apart on ungreased baking sheets. Bake for 13 to 15 minutes, until the cookies are golden brown and have spread. Bake the cookies in batches if necessary. Let the cookies cool on the baking sheets on wire cooling racks for about 5 minutes before removing them with a wide spatula and transferring them to the cooling racks to cool completely.

CHOCOLATE CUPCAKES WITH PEANUT BUTTER–MASCARPONE FROSTING

Cake mixes are great things. I like to bake cakes from scratch, but when I don't have the time, I rely on cake mixes and dress them up with amazing frosting. This recipe uses two of my favorite frosting ingredients: creamy peanut butter and even creamier mascarpone cheese. Peanut butter and chocolate is a classic combination, as anyone who has ever tasted a Reese's Peanut Butter Cup can attest to. Mascarpone is no trickier to work with than cream cheese, and yet it is richer and even more luscious. Mix the two together and slather them on top of the chocolate cupcakes, and you're in for a luscious treat. I promise. If you prefer to make a layer cake with the mix, there's ample frosting for that.

Makes 24 cupcakes

- 1 standard-size box chocolate cake mix
- 1 cup mascarpone cheese
- ¼ cup creamy peanut butter
- ¼ cup apple juice
- 3 tablespoons heavy cream
- Pinch of salt
- One 1-pound box confectioners' sugar
- ½ cup chopped salted peanuts

TO PREPARE: Bake the cupcakes according to the cake mix package directions. Let them cool completely on a wire rack.

In the bowl of a standing mixer fitted with the paddle attachment and set on medium-high speed, beat the mascarpone until creamy. Add the peanut butter and mix until creamy. Add the apple juice, heavy cream, and salt and beat until smooth.

With the mixer on low speed, gradually beat in the confectioners' sugar. Continue mixing until the frosting is smooth and creamy.

Using a spatula, frost the cupcakes liberally with the frosting. Top with the peanuts.

WHAT IS MASCARPONE CHEESE?

I am in love with this thick, rich, outrageously creamy cheese. It's a fresh Italian cheese made from heavy, sweet cream, and while its texture is similar to the best cream cheese you've ever tasted, its flavor far exceeds it. *Smooth*, *luxurious*, *velvety*, and *lush* are words that can be applied. I love to blend mascarpone with both sweet and savory flavors. It is sold in tubs in cheese shops, specialty stores, and many supermarkets with well-stocked cheese counters.

SMOOTH, LUXURIOUS, VELVETY, **AND** ***LUSH*** **ARE WORDS THAT CAN BE APPLIED. I LOVE TO BLEND MASCARPONE WITH BOTH SWEET AND SAVORY FLAVORS.**

TIRAMISU CUPCAKES

When you stir mascarpone into the batter, what might be an ordinary cupcake instantly evolves into a decadent one. Rich, triple-cream mascarpone cheese is a luxury well worth indulging in every now and then. It's the telling ingredient in tiramisu, one of my favorite desserts, and so I decided to use it in a cupcake for portable tiramisu. Carry a batch of these along and you'll be welcome anywhere you go!

Makes 24 cupcakes

CUPCAKE FILLING:

1 cup mascarpone cheese
3 tablespoons coffee liqueur, such as Tia Maria or Kahlúa
¼ cup sweetened condensed milk
One 8-ounce container Cool Whip

CUPCAKES:

One 18.25-ounce box white cake mix
½ cup confectioners' sugar
¾ cup hot brewed coffee
1 tablespoon pure vanilla extract

FROSTING:

One 8-ounce package cream cheese, softened
½ cup (1 stick) unsalted butter, softened
1 teaspoon pure vanilla extract
White chocolate liqueur, such as Godiva
2 cups confectioners' sugar
Dark chocolate shavings, for garnish

TO MAKE THE CUPCAKE FILLING: In a large bowl and using a handheld mixer set on medium speed, beat together the mascarpone, coffee liqueur, and condensed milk until smooth and blended. Using a rubber spatula, fold in the Cool Whip. Cover and refrigerate for at least 4 hours and up to 6 hours.

TO MAKE THE CUPCAKES: Meanwhile, bake cupcakes according to the cake mix package directions. Let cool on a wire cooling rack.

In a medium bowl, stir the confectioners' sugar into the hot coffee until the sugar dissolves. Stir in the vanilla.

recipe continued on page 212

TO MAKE THE FROSTING: In a large bowl and using a handheld mixer set on medium speed, beat the cream cheese and butter for 2 to 3 minutes, until light and fluffy. Mix in the vanilla and chocolate liqueur. With the mixer on low speed, slowly add the confectioners' sugar to the frosting until it reaches a spreadable consistency.

TO FILL AND FROST THE CUPCAKES: Using a fork, pierce the cupcakes several times and brush each one liberally with the sweetened coffee.

Spoon the mascarpone mixture into a pastry bag fitted with a plain tip and inject small amounts directly into the center of each cupcake. The best way to do this is to insert the pastry bag tip into the top of the cupcakes.

Using a spatula, frost the cupcakes liberally with the frosting and garnish with chocolate shavings.

RICH, TRIPLE-CREAM MASCARPONE CHEESE IS A LUXURY WELL WORTH INDULGING IN EVERY NOW AND THEN.

ORZO PUDDING

This is my idea of rice pudding, but of course it's made with orzo (a pasta), which cooks far more quickly, and you don't run the risk of undercooking or overcooking the rice. Otherwise, it's pretty classic, down to the cinnamon and raisins.

Serves 4 to 6

5 cups heavy cream
1 cup sugar
3 tablespoons pure vanilla extract
1 teaspoon ground cinnamon
One 1-pound box orzo
1½ cups raisins, optional
Whipped cream, for garnish, optional
3 pints mixed fresh berries, such as strawberries, raspberries, blackberries, or blueberries, or a mixture of any of these

TO PREPARE: In a large pot, bring the heavy cream to a simmer over medium heat. Add the orzo, sugar, vanilla, and cinnamon and cook, stirring frequently, until smooth and creamy, about 30 minutes, or until tender and the pudding is a desirable consistency. Stir in the raisins and remove the saucepan from the heat.

Transfer to a bowl, cover, cool to room temperature, and then refrigerate for at least 2 hours and up to 4 hours. Serve with whipped cream, if desired, and berries. You can serve this pudding cold, directly from the refrigerator, or serve it warm. To warm it up, heat it in the microwave for 30 seconds, then stir and heat for another 30 seconds.

WHITE CHOCOLATE PUDDING

I was fooling around with white chocolate chips one day and came up with this. It's sort of a surprise because it's white but not vanilla flavored (although the vanilla bean enhances the white chocolate). With the sliced strawberries, I like this dessert for Valentine's Day.

Serves 6

4 large egg yolks

2 tablespoons cornstarch

1 quart heavy cream

⅔ cup sugar

2 tablespoons pure vanilla extract

1 cup white chocolate chips

Milk chocolate shavings, for garnish

Sliced fresh strawberries, for garnish

TO PREPARE: In a small bowl, beat together the egg yolks and cornstarch until well mixed. Set aside.

In a large saucepan, mix together the heavy cream, sugar, and vanilla and heat over medium-high heat until the cream begins to boil; do not let the cream boil over.

Decrease the heat to low and stir in the chocolate chips. Cook, stirring, until the chips melt completely, 2 to 3 minutes.

Spoon about 4 tablespoons of the hot cream–chocolate chip mixture into the beaten eggs and whisk well to temper the eggs (this will prevent the egg yolks from curdling). Add the tempered eggs to the hot cream–chocolate chip mixture and simmer over medium heat until the custard thickens, about 1 minute.

Remove the saucepan from the heat and pour the custard into a 1½-quart, heat-safe glass serving dish. Let cool in the refrigerator for at least 4 hours to let it thicken and chill thoroughly.

Serve the pudding garnished with milk chocolate shavings and sliced strawberries.

CINNAMON-PEACH BREAD PUDDING

A lot of folks think of Georgia as having great peaches, but New Jersey grows some of the best in the nation. This is why when I decided to make a bread pudding with fruit, I immediately thought of peaches. I make a wicked chocolate chip and banana bread pudding and so knew I could [illegible] ke this one equally delicious, and maybe better. I also recommend this puddin [illegible] summertime, when peaches are at their juicy peak. If you crave bre [illegible] intertime, I recommend frozen peaches.

d biscuits (in a tube)

cinnamon rolls (in a tube)

ened

sliced peaches, thawed (1-pound bag,

sed milk

rolls according to the package directions.
ng packet. Let the biscuits and rolls cool
ch cubes.
he peach preserves and set aside.
glass or ceramic baking dish with the

ared baking dish so that they cover

nd then pour over the bread cubes
in [illegible] d cubes and peaches are evenly
mi [illegible] ad-peach mixture.
I [illegible] densed milk, and eggs until well
mix [illegible]
Ba [illegible] a small knife inserted near the
cente [illegible] om the oven and top with small dollops
of the [illegible] bread pudding cool slightly before serving.

BUTTERMILK DOUGHNUTS WITH BLUEBERRY COMPOTE

These are not your ordinary doughnuts. You would never be tempted to dunk one in a cup of coffee but instead will want a knife and fork to eat them. Like all doughnuts, these are fried, which makes them especially delicious, and while it's an effort to make them, try it. Nothing beats eating hot, just-fried doughnuts, and these, with their light lemony flavor and jammy sauce, are out of this world.

Serves 8 to 12

BLUEBERRY COMPOTE:

2½ cups fresh blueberries
¼ cup sugar
Juice of 1 lemon
Grated zest of 1 lemon

DOUGHNUTS:

2 tablespoons vegetable shortening, such as Crisco
2 tablespoons mascarpone cheese
½ cup sugar
1 large egg
½ teaspoon pure vanilla extract
⅔ cup buttermilk
2 cups all-purpose flour
½ teaspoon baking soda
Pinch of salt
Canola oil, for frying
Confectioners' sugar, for dusting the doughnuts

TO MAKE THE COMPOTE: In a small saucepan, mix together 2 cups of the blueberries, the sugar, and 2 tablespoons water and bring to a simmer over medium-high heat. Simmer until the compote is syrupy and the blueberries begin to break down, 5 to 6 minutes.

Transfer the compote to the bowl of a food processor fitted with the metal blade, add the lemon juice, and pulse until smooth. Put the compote in a bowl and garnish with the reserved ½ cup berries and the lemon zest.

TO MAKE THE DOUGHNUTS: In the bowl of a standing mixer fitted with the paddle attachment and set on medium speed, beat together the shortening, mascarpone, and sugar until smooth and well blended.

In a large glass measuring cup, whisk together the egg and vanilla. With the mixer on medium speed, add the egg to the batter, and then add the buttermilk.

Sift together the flour, baking soda, and salt. With the mixer on low speed, slowly add the flour mixture to the batter until incorporated into a dough.

On a lightly floured surface, roll the dough out into a round about ⅓ inch thick. Using a 2½-inch biscuit or doughnut cutter, punch out 16 to 24 doughnuts. Let the doughnuts rest for about 10 minutes.

Meanwhile, in a deep-fat fryer or deep, heavy pot, heat enough oil to reach a depth of 3 to 4 inches to 375°F.

Using long-handled tongs, submerge 2 or 3 doughnuts at a time (to avoid crowding) in the hot oil, and when they bob to the surface, let them fry until golden brown, about 2 minutes. Turn and let them fry on the other side until golden brown, about 2 minutes longer. Let the oil regain its temperature between batches.

Carefully lift the doughnuts from the hot oil and drain on paper towels. Dust with confectioners' sugar and serve warm with the compote.

NOTHING BEATS EATING HOT, JUST-FRIED DOUGHNUTS, AND THESE ARE OUT OF THIS WORLD.

VANILLA ICE CREAM SUNDAES WITH HOMEMADE BUTTERSCOTCH SAUCE AND SWEETENED VANILLA WHIPPED CREAM

Ice cream sundaes are usually a hit with everyone, and it's fun to build your own at home. This one reminds me of the days when my older son, Josh, was a little guy and he and I liked to visit an ice cream parlor called Holiday Lakes in Edgewater Park, New Jersey. Both of us were in love with the butterscotch sauce—and it's still our favorite.

Serves 4

BUTTERSCOTCH SAUCE:

- ¾ cup butterscotch chips
- ½ cup heavy cream
- 1 tablespoon (½ ounce) Scotch whisky

SWEETENED VANILLA WHIPPED CREAM:

- 1 cup heavy cream
- ¼ cup confectioners' sugar
- 1 teaspoon pure vanilla extract

SUNDAES:

- 1 quart vanilla ice cream

TO MAKE THE SAUCE: Put the butterscotch chips in a large stainless steel or heat-safe glass bowl.

In a small, heavy saucepan, heat the heavy cream and whisky over medium-high heat, stirring constantly, just until the mixture begins to boil, 3 to 4 minutes; do not let the cream boil over. Pour the cream over the butterscotch chips and whisk well until smooth and velvety. Set aside, covered, to keep warm.

TO MAKE THE WHIPPED CREAM: In the bowl of a standing mixer fitted with the whisk attachment, combine the heavy cream, confectioners' sugar, and vanilla. With the mixer on low speed, beat until smooth. Gradually increase the mixer's speed to high and beat until the cream forms stiff peaks, 2 to 3 minutes.

TO MAKE THE SUNDAES: Spoon 2 scoops of ice cream into each of 4 sundae dishes. Ladle 2 to 4 tablespoons of the butterscotch sauce over the ice cream and top with the whipped cream. (If the butterscotch sauce is no longer fluid enough, heat it in a microwave on high power for about 1 minute.)

APPLE-PEAR COBBLER

I usually have apples and pears in the kitchen in the fall, when they are at their best, and one day I decided to make this cobbler. There's not more of a story attached to this recipe, but it's really good, just what you want from a cobbler. Sweetened vanilla whipped cream (see page 218) dolloped on top would make it even better.

Serves 8 to 10

2 cups diced Anjou, Bosc, or Bartlett pears (about 1 pound)
2 cups diced tart apples (about 1 pound)
1 cup packed dark brown sugar
2 tablespoons pear nectar
½ cup (1 stick) unsalted butter, softened
1 cup sugar
¾ cup self-rising flour
2 teaspoons baking powder
1 teaspoon ground cinnamon
¼ teaspoon salt
¾ cup milk
1 large egg
1½ cups of your favorite granola

TO PREPARE: Preheat the oven to 325°F.

In a large bowl, toss the pears and apples with the brown sugar and pear nectar.

Put the butter in a 9-inch square casserole dish, and put the dish in the oven until the butter melts.

In a medium bowl, mix together the sugar, flour, baking powder, cinnamon, and salt.

In a large bowl, whisk together the milk and egg. Slowly whisk the dry ingredient mixture into the milk-egg mixture to make a batter.

Pour the batter into the casserole with the melted butter. Spoon the pears and apples over the batter; do not stir.

Bake for 50 minutes. Remove the cobbler from the oven and top with the granola. Return to the oven and bake for about 10 minutes longer, or until the fruit is tender and the top of the cobbler is nicely browned. Serve warm or at room temperature.

SPICY CHOCOLATE-CHERRY TRUFFLES

"OMG!" was all I heard from my wife, Kimberly, and my sister Vang when they tasted these truffles. Neither had thought they would like chocolate and spices together, but they were happily surprised. If ever there was a "hot and poppin'" dessert, this is it!

Makes about 16 truffles

- **8 ounces semisweet chocolate, finely chopped**
- **½ cup plus 2 tablespoons heavy cream**
- **¼ cup brewed coffee**
- **1 teaspoon cayenne pepper**
- **One 12-ounce can cherry pie filling, drained and diced**
- **½ cup graham cracker crumbs**
- **¼ cup unsweetened cocoa powder**

TO PREPARE: Put the chocolate in a large bowl and set aside. Have a larger bowl filled with cold water and ice ready. Line a baking sheet or sheet pan with parchment paper.

In a medium saucepan, bring the heavy cream, coffee, and cayenne to a boil over medium-high heat. Stir in the cherry filling. Pour the hot mixture over the chocolate and whisk until the chocolate melts and the mixture is as smooth as possible.

Set the bowl over the larger bowl filled with cold water and ice and whisk until the chocolate begins to harden. Refrigerate for about 10 minutes, and then scoop about 1½ tablespoons of the chocolate mixture onto the prepared baking sheet. Between dampened palms, roll the mound of chocolate into a ball about 1 inch in diameter. Repeat with the rest of the chocolate. If the chocolate softens while you work, return the bowl to the refrigerator to firm up the chocolate a little.

Mix together the graham cracker crumbs and cocoa powder and spread in a shallow dish or plate. Roll the truffles in the crumbs until well coated and return to the baking sheet. Return the truffles to the refrigerator and let them harden for at least 4 hours and up to 2 days.

INDEX

D

E-F

G

H

I-K

L-M

N-O

P

Q-R

S

T

V-Z